First published in 2021 by Ichtheon on Amazon KDP

This paperback edition published in 2021 by Ichtheon, c/o Harbottle & Lewis LLP, 7 Savoy Court, London WC2R 0EX

ISBN: 9798500589590

A CIP catalogue record for this book is available from The British Library.

4 3 2 1

Typeset in Adobe Garamond Premier Pro.

for the love of fish

an aquarist's journey

Robert Porter

to my **family**

Table of contents

Foreword by Lord Smith of Finsbury 2

Chapter 1: Introduction 3

Chapter 2: The benefits of fishkeeping 5

Chapter 3: Beginnings 8

Chapter 4: The experimental tank 12

Chapter 5: The invocation of an obsession and tropical freshwater fish in art and literature 26

Chapter 6: Tropical freshwater fish and conservation....................41

Chapter 7: The beautiful fish: a loving profile of the zebra danio............ 51

Chapter 8: Planning for a bigger tank 56

Chapter 9: Preparing for a Danio Dreamworld.................... 62

Chapter 10: Aquascaping and biotope integrity 69

Chapter 11: Cats, lateral lines, bagpipes and hoovers................. 72

Chapter 12: Top Tips.. 76

Chapter 13: Conclusion... 91

Chapter 14: Appendices 93

Appendix 1: Robert's 240-litre tank list (for fishless cycling) 94

Appendix 2: The illegality of fish-in cycling under the Animal Welfare Act 2006.. 96

Appendix 3: Irish Times Amazon article (2021) 102

Appendix 4: Early draft of Tropical Fish Hobbyist Magazine article 105

Appendix 5: Taxonomy of fish species populating 240-litre tank............. 110

Appendix 6: The history of aquariums: A general timeline 111

Select bibliography 117

List of images 118

List of figures..119

Acknowledgements 120

About the author 122

Editorial note

In this book, the scientific names of fish, invertebrates and plants are given on the first occasion they occur, but not necessarily thereafter.

Foreword
by Lord Smith of Finsbury

I have to confess to being a bit of a fraud in writing this foreword. I have never been a fishkeeper, have never owned an aquarium, and know very little about the joy of keeping and looking after fish. Once when I was staying in a friend's house whilst he and his family were away, and in charge of the fish tank, I over-fed them (something specifically warned about in Robert's Chapter 12) and the result was a disaster. So I'm not really the right person to write a Foreword. But when my good friend Robert asked me to do so, I said yes and here I am. But in a way I *am* the right person to be writing this, because – having read *For the Love of Fish* with delight and fascination – I realise that you don't have to be a dedicated aquarist to relish and enjoy this book. It's a book for everyone, fishkeeper and non-fishkeeper alike.

It is a tale, beautifully and engagingly written, of Robert's developing love and experience of fishkeeping, through his life, and the lessons and delights he finds along the way. The non-expert will marvel at the complexities of getting the right filter, the right balance of ammonia and nitrite, the right landscaping, the right care when moving house, the right number of fish. The enthusiast will find tips in abundance. And we will all find and share Robert's joy over his beloved zebra danios.

Above all, this book is full of fun. It tells us, having set up our aquarium with all the care and attention to detail that we need to devote to the process, to sit back and have a beer and marvel at the beauty of what we see. It warns us that – whilst hoovering a deep-pile carpet may not disturb the fish – practising the bagpipes most certainly will. Go and play them somewhere else.

There is also, in a final appendix, a fascinating history of aquariums, dating back four and a half millennia to Sumerian times. And there is a passionate cry for the importance of biodiversity and its role in the sustenance of humanity and of our planet, not only in a well-targeted appendix about the Amazon, but in the concluding section of the book itself. The closing perception speaks of tropical freshwater fish in a compelling way: "They are also a part of God's Creation and glorify God through the very fact they are fish and through their role as our pets. As a result, they demand our compassion, respect and safeguarding." It's a salutary reminder that the whole fragile biodiversity of our earth demands our compassion, respect and safeguarding.

Chris Smith, May 2021

1

Introduction

"Eventually every aquarium will leak". This witty observation from Edward A. Murphy Jr seemingly warns us off a pastime that has the capability of bringing us great knowledge and pleasure.

Nevertheless, it is best to dive into the aquarist's pursuit in full awareness that things can – and do – sometimes go wrong. As with most occurrences in life, it is not the fact that things go wrong that determines outcomes, but how we deal with problems when they surface. On a level, the aquarist's art is primarily a function of common sense once a number of basic scientific and practical principles are learnt.

It is not the function of this book to be a handbook of everything an aquarist needs to know successfully to pursue the hobby. I have kept fish on and off since

Leopard danio *(Danio rerio)*

I was a teenager, but I have only managed a handful of fish tanks, and I cannot compete with those who have spent the whole of their lives doing so or have spent twenty years working in an aquarium shop. If you are looking for an aquarium manual, then look elsewhere. This is a subjective account, written from a personal perspective.

What I do have, then, is a story to tell. When I first kept tropical freshwater fish in the early 1980s, the notion of testing for ammonia and nitrite was foreign and the domain of marine saltwater fishkeepers. Thirty years later (as I will explain in detail in a subsequent chapter), the whole environment had changed.

This book is a consolidated journal of my teenage days as an aquarist in the 1980s and my more recent resurrection as a contemporary fishkeeper. It is my hope that this approach will be of general light-hearted interest to other aquarists as well as to those who are considering dipping their toe in the water, or who have dedicated fishkeepers in their family and just want to know what all the fuss is about.

Despite this approach, along the way I also impart opinions based on some hard-learned lessons from my experiences, in the hope they will be of interest and might save others some heartache along the way.

I do not enter into very detailed discussions about the possibilities around aquarium equipment or the vagaries of the nitrogen cycle (although I do discuss them a little). It seems to me there are plenty of books out there dealing with all this, and they almost certainly discuss it more eloquently and with more experience than I could.

Equally, I do not set out an exhaustive or detailed analysis of fish or plant species that might be suitable for a community – or even a specialist biotope – tank, because I am neither a zoologist nor an experienced ichthyologist; and, again, other books deal with this in considerable detail. The one exception to this is my analysis of some species of Danios, in which I take a particular interest.

So, this book is primarily a story with lessons attached. It might, if I were going to be pretentious (which I suppose I am), be a sort of *Canterbury Tales* for aquarists – a darn good yarn with some didactic purpose attached. Thankfully, you will be delighted to know, it is not written in Chaucerian English.

It is to be enjoyed. I hope you enjoy it!

2

The benefits of fishkeeping

Can you fall in love with a fish? I mean, in the same way that you can fall in love with your dog or your cat? It's an interesting question. Many fish don't live more than three or four years, and typically fish occasionally die on you, especially if you opt for fish-in cycling (see Chapter 4) and send out "suicide squads" of hardy fish to populate your tank while the bacteria in your filter and substrate are developing and the nitrogen cycle is cycling.

For that reason alone it might be unwise to fall in love with your fish. But, speaking for myself, while I may not love my fish with the same intensity as I love my cats, I certainly do love them. Even though I specialise in shoaling fish, I rarely keep a shoal of more than eight specimens of any one species, so that each fish is capable of becoming a little character of its own. While they cannot sit on my lap

Cardinal tetras in shoal *(Paracheirodon axelrodi)*

like my cat, and I cannot take them for walks like a dog, they keep me company and entice me into the splendour of their watery world.

One friend of mine once told me that she could never keep fish because fish were meant for eating, like salmon or cod. This put me in mind of frying up my little shoal of zebra danios and eating them in batter like whitebait. The difference is, of course, that no-one keeps salmon or cod as pets. But when you keep tropical freshwater fish in an aquarium they *are* pets. And they must be treated as such. Does anyone ever fall in love with a salmon or a cod? I doubt it.

That said, the recent documentary *My Octopus Teacher* (Netflix), which won Best Documentary at the 2021 Academy Awards, and which follows the love affair of a man with his octopus, might suggest that humanity is capable of falling in love not just with vertebrates, but also certain invertebrates. I suppose this argues strongly for the suggestion that *anything* kept as a pet is capable of being loved. I have never heard of a salmon or cod being kept as a pet (however, see Appendix 6, where the development of fishponds in aquaculture led eventually to more ornamental uses), but there is no doubt that a huge plethora of tropical freshwater fish species are so kept.

More than this, if you get the Aquascaping right, the watery world of topical freshwater fish can be quite magical and can welcome you into a specific biotope that glorifies God's creation.

So no, I don't think it is likely you can form a deep bond with a fish the same way that you can with a dog or a cat. But you can still love them. Of course there are those who would argue that this is a hopeless exercise because fish cannot love you back. That might be true to an extent, but what fishkeeper doesn't imagine when they put their fingers into the tank at feeding time that the fish know intuitively who you are and what you are doing? For that moment the fish are yours – they belong to you and they respond to you as to no other.

So, these are the first two benefits of fishkeeping: an exercise in love, and in glorifying God's creation.

There are plenty of others. Why, for instance, are fish tanks so prevalent in doctors' and dentists' waiting rooms? Precisely because they are good for you. Gazing at a fish tank calms the mind and is a tonic for the soul. Who couldn't be mesmerised by a flitting shoal of cardinal tetras (*Paracheirodon axelrodi*) or by the incessant bobbing of a pearl gourami (*Trichopodus leerii*)? How many anxious boys and girls with aching molars have been calmed and reassured by the dentist's aquarium?

Beyond this lies another tonic for the soul. To be a good fishkeeper, you have to master a number of technical and scientific aspects. To my mind there are three types of these. First there are the technical elements around mastering equipment such as filters, tanks, wave makers, heaters, syphons, etc. Secondly there are the technical aspects around water quality that focus around the nitrogen cycle such as pH, gH, kH, ammonia, nitrite and nitrate. And finally there are what I might call the zoological and ichthyological aspects of fishkeeping, where it is important to master details of fish and plant species and fish physiology.

In this respect being an aquarist is something like being a scuba diver. I dived for many years in my twenties and thirties, and one of the things that struck me about it was the fact that managing the equipment and the technical aspects of diving were almost as important as the act of submerging itself. You were always comparing and assessing the latest BCD (Stab Jacket) or regulator or wrist-worn dive computer. If you wanted to get into the marine biology and zoology of the fishes there was plenty of scope for that, too, and PADI runs speciality courses in this regard.

It's the same for fishkeeping: mastering the equipment and technicalities is almost as important as keeping the fish themselves, and – perhaps surprisingly – equally as enjoyable. Indeed, just as you couldn't dive safely without mastering the equipment, you can't keep fish competently and with the fishes' welfare in mind without doing the same.

This can all seem quite daunting at first, but there are plenty of books out there to help you learn; why not start with *The Perfect Aquarium* by Jeremy Gay, and *Practical Fishkeeping's The Aquarium Masterclass?* Equally, magazines such as *Practical Fishkeeping* and *Tropical Fish Hobbyist* can help lead the way. For myself, acquiring all this knowledge and learning all these skills gave me a sense of great pride and fulfilment.

Moreover, learning about fish is a joy in itself. I will discuss in Chapter 10 how important it is to create a meaningful Aquascape, and within that ideally a biotope, that has integrity in the context of the species you intend to keep. Learning about the needs of each species – their needs and wants and how they interact with their environment and other species – is a joy in itself. Creating a biotope that enables your fish to thrive can be a source of great pride.

It's at this point my heart glows and I realise that, like a great operatic voice soaring to the Heavens, a well-Aquascaped and maintained fish tank is a thing of beauty and is a joy for ever.

If that's not a benefit of keeping fish, then I don't know what is.

3

Beginnings

When I was fourteen I had my first publishing success. A letter of mine was printed by Brian Whiteside in the "What is Your Opinion?" column of *The Aquarist and Pondkeeper* magazine.

Here's the relevant excerpt from the August 1980 edition:

I was pleased to receive the following letter from a young aquarist who lives in Northern Ireland because despite the fact there are many expert aquarists in Northern Ireland few ever write in to this feature. Master Robert Porter is fourteen years of age and lives... [in] Belfast. He says "I was interested to read in the April [1980] edition of *Aquarist and Pondkeeper* about Mrs Shuttle and her pH saga. I have had a similar experience.

Over a year ago when I first set up my tank, I purchased a pH test kit and adjusted the pH in the tank religiously. Soon after I was informed by an experienced aquarist that he had never tested the pH in his life and that all his fish were thriving. So I began to test the pH less frequently and eventually only if the fish looked distressed. I have a pair of *Mollienesia sphenops* that were admired by another experienced aquarist; and though I say it myself they are both exceedingly beautiful – and even more so when in breeding condition. Although black mollies are very hardy they do best, as they say, in alkaline water.

About three days before I read Mrs Shuttle's letter my male dwarf gourami died of a severe case of dropsy and, as a precaution I changed one third of the water and tested the pH. Horrors! Like Mrs Shuttle's the pH of my tank was around 6.0 – far too low for the ideal community aquarium; and my mollies should have been very uncomfortable. To raise the pH a little I did not reduce the alkalinity of my replacement water and this brought up the pH to a more acceptable level. Luckily, unlike Mrs Shuttle's, my fish did not suffer any ill-effects from the change in pH.

Black moly *(Poecilia sphenops)*

What of my mollies? In those water conditions they should have been showing some signs of distress, which they were not – although occasionally they develop white blotches on their bodies; but these do not normally last longer than a few days. The female is especially prone to these. What are they?

Is pH, for tank-bred specimens, all that important? I don't pretend to answer that question because I'm not experienced enough; but perhaps in a few years' time, with more knowledge and more experience with different species of fish, I will be able to form my own conclusions.

Certainly, I have no fish which it is considered a tremendous feat to keep successfully – although I like to think I have a wide variety of catfish for a community aquarium. They include pepper cat, schwartz cat, porthole cat, leopard cat, sucking cat and five striped cats; and of the loaches coolie loaches and clown loach.

However I do intend to rectify the pH problem – bicarbonate of soda here we come! – and to stop it recurring. Do you have any helpful suggestions as to what caused the build-up of acidity?"

I remember being castigated for this letter by the proprietors of Grosvenor Aquatics on the Woodstock Road in Belfast because they said they could have answered my questions rather than writing in to Brian Whiteside. But I had one over on them. Already interested in becoming a barrister as my profession, I had been told that in cross-examination you never asked a question to which you did not already know the answer: so I already knew the answers (or most of them) to the questions I had posited. For instance, the build up in acidity was almost certainly caused by the fact I wasn't cleaning detritus from the substrate frequently enough because in those days I thought that my under-gravel filter would deal with the problem.

The question I asked about the importance of pH for tank-bred specimens is interesting: although I have not thoroughly researched the issue, I am aware that tank-bred *Corydoras* may be more tolerant of higher pH levels than wild-caught specimens. Perhaps I will address this question in more depth in future.

It was, nevertheless, deeply satisfying to have my letter published in *The Aquarist and Pondkeeper*, and it was a testament to how seriously I was taking fishkeeping at such a tender age.

My dad bought me a 24"x15"x12" glass tank with metal edges for my thirteenth birthday. I set it up with an under-gravel filter (very in vogue in those days) with the suction drawing down into the gravel rather than up through it. I also had a Rena internal filter and an air pump and air stone. It was all set for an intensely stocked community tank.

Now in those days few aquarists had heard about the nitrogen cycle, ammonia and nitrite levels in the context of tropical freshwater fishkeeping. It was all about pH, nitrate and CO_2 levels. For instance, probably the most influential textbook of the time, *All About Tropical Fish* by Derek McInerny and Geoffrey Gerard (1980), has no mention of the nitrogen cycle, ammonia or nitrite in its index.

So, oblivious to such concerns, I stocked my tank with mollies, guppies (*Poecilia reticulata*), Siamese fighting fish (*Betta splendens*), zebra danios (*Danio rerio*) and neon tetras (*Paracheirodon innesi*) – and of course quite a few *Corydoras* catfish! – and looked on happily at my display. It was a long time ago, and my recollection may be hazy (I did not keep an aquarist's notebook back then), but I don't remember having many casualties in the early part of my fishkeeping career. By rights, though, my fish should have been regularly floating dead to the surface because goodness knows what the ammonia and nitrite levels were while my filters were establishing bacteria.

It's not even as if my tank was heavily planted, because as you can imagine my under-gravel filter meant that my plants had difficulty establishing.

Anyhow, it was a miracle all my fish didn't die. When more recently I set up my experimental 40-litre tank, I mentioned this fact to the manager of the shop where I bought my fish for it. He said he thought that in-breeding had made fish less robust than thirty years ago, and also perhaps deteriorated water quality made them less hardy.

Anyway, my fishkeeping in the 1980s went from strength to strength. I bought pearl gouramis (*Trichopodus leerii*) and a red-tailed black shark (*Epalzeorhynchos bicolor*) that prowled behind my filter and a beautiful ram cichlid (*Mikrogeophagus ramirezi*) that thrived for many years. My favourite fish were two gorgeous pepper corydoras (*Corydoras paleatus*). The smaller of them had only one eye (I'm not sure how he lost one) and he had a beautiful spirit.

Soon I took to breeding. I bought a small plastic breeding tank that I could hang off the edge of the main tank, and there I successfully bred guppies, black mollies and zebra danios.

It's safe to say that in my teens my fishkeeping was a substantial success. In 1984, however, I went to university, and so could not look after my tank with the requisite diligence. At about the same time my parents moved house. Disaster struck. Since my parents were downsizing considerably, they held an auction of some of the items in the house. Someone bought the living-room carpet. Someone else bought my fish tank. That person tried to lift the fish tank into the boot of their car without first emptying it of water. Well, you can imagine: shattered glass, fish writhing all over the floor, a ruined carpet. I was not there to witness it myself, but the event went down in the annals of family folklore.

And thus ended my assignation with tropical freshwater fish for thirty years.

4

The experimental tank

Our family has two beautiful cats. About once every six weeks I go to Pets at Home to buy wet and dry cat food and cat litter. One day about a year ago I chose to wander through the store and I happened across the fish tanks. A feeling of great reminiscence came over me as I gazed at the neon tetras before me. And as my eyes focussed in on the beautiful horizontal blue and silver lines of the darting zebra danios, suddenly I felt a deep urge that I had not felt in over thirty years – the urge to keep fish.

Before I left the store, I bought Jeremy Gay's *The Perfect Aquarium*, and I began to read it that night in the bath (all the best books are begun in the bath, I find!). Within fifteen minutes I was hooked.

But something niggled at me. There was lots of talk in the book about tank cycling, the nitrogen cycle and ammonia and nitrite levels. All of this was foreign to me. Was my memory deceiving me, or was this all new? I foraged through my

Green cabomba *(Cabomba caroliniana)*

A typical crypt *(Cryptocoryne wendtii)*

bookshelf and found the favourite fishkeeping book of my youth – *All About Tropical Fish*. I flicked through it. There was no mention of the nitrogen cycle, ammonia or nitrite at all. Had the hobby moved on so much?

A brief chat with David, the manager of the Pets at Home store where I most regularly shop, convinced me that it had. I realised immediately that I had a great deal to learn and that it would be wise to take baby steps towards a larger 240-litre tank which I had initially had my eye on. I decided, therefore, to purchase a smaller 40-litre tank that I could use as a learning experiment, and also co-incidentally persuade my wife that tropical fishkeeping was a nice thing to do, because I wasn't convinced that she would automatically fall into line.

Figure 1: Equipment[1] purchased for experimental 40-litre tank and its cycling

40-litre tank	Siphon
Filter	Algae sponge
Swop-out filter (Fluval U2)	Curved scissors and spatulas
Heater	Substrate Soil and Plants
LED lighting rig	Dr Tim's One and Only
Fish flakes	Dr Tim's First Defense
Bacterial enhancer (Fluval)	Tapsafe
Net	Plant fertiliser (Tropica Premium Nutrition)

1   Always be sure to read equipment instructions carefully, and to take particular care when handling electrical equipment. Remember that water and electricity present a particular hazard.

It was at this point that I dived into as many aquarists' books and manuals as I could find. Foremost amongst these were, as I say, *The Perfect Aquarium*, but also *Practical Fishkeeping*'s *The Aquarium Masterclass*, and two more specialist books, both of which I will repeatedly refer to again: *The Ecology of the Planted Aquarium* by Diana Walstad and *Aquascaping* by George Farmer. I also took out annual subscriptions to both *Practical Fishkeeping* and *Tropical Fish Hobbyist* magazines and began to read them avidly.

I spent three days negotiating with my wife to put a 40-litre tank in the bedroom, and after succeeding in that, I went back to Pets at Home and bought my tank, which came complete with a filter and a heater. I also bought dechlorinator, a net, a syphon, some plant fertiliser, some fish flakes and some Fluval biological enhancer. Later that morning I set up my tank and left it overnight. The next day I went to another specialist aquatics store in London and bought some aquatic plants – green cabomba (*Cabomba caroliniana*), two types of *Cryptocoryne*, an Amazon sword plant (*Echinodorus bleheri*) and some vallisneria (*Vallisneria americana*). I rushed home and planted my 40-litre tank up and doused it with fertiliser and biological enhancer. It looked beautiful almost immediately, and I settled in for a week to let the filter begin to mature.

It was at this point I made a number of mistakes. The first of these was the most serious. The filter I bought with my 40-litre tank was very cheap, and it was in fact substandard for three reasons. First, the water flow from the filter was not powerful enough to provide good filtration, even for a tank as small as 40 litres. Secondly, the top of the part of the filter that housed the filter media was transparent, which arguably means that bacteria do not grow as fast in the media because they prefer darkness. And thirdly – and most crucially – the translucent top of the filter was not a snug fit and had wide slats, which meant that smaller fish could wriggle their way into the filter.

I eventually lost three Danios that way, and soon I had to bite the bullet and swop out the substandard filter for an internal Fluval U2, which has worked wonders to this day. The trouble was that the filter media between the filters was not compatible, so I had to start my cycling all over again, which lost me a month.

This last point was extremely relevant to my second mistake. I

Amazon sword plant (*Echinodorus bleheri*)

had been encouraged by a retailer to do fish-in cycling. Fish-in cycling is very alluring because it means that you can stock your tank with a few fish within a week of setting up your tank. But it means that you use the fish as a source of ammonia to kick-start the nitrogen cycling, and that they have to endure adverse water conditions, including high spikes in ammonia and nitrite while you wait for the filter and the tank to mature.

By the time I realised my mistake – which was exacerbated by the necessity to swop out my substandard filter – I was fully committed, and I realised that the little group of zebra danios I had joyfully bought, expecting nothing but the best for them, was in fact transformed into a "suicide squad".

I watched as my Danios hugged the bottom of the tank in lethargy and one of them died (having already lost three to my substandard filter). Ammonia and nitrite levels spiked at 4ppm each. At this point I dug in. Determined to rescue my fish, I committed to 25% water changes daily until cycling was complete. It was relentless, and it took five weeks, even with a healthy dose of live bacteria (there are several on the market but I opted for Dr Tim's One and Only).

Even within that regimen I kept making smallish mistakes. My pH was down to 6.0, and eventually I realised that if I brought it up to 7.0 the bacteria would grow more quickly. Equally, bacteria grow quicker in warmer water, but because I had stocked my tank with zebra danios I had to keep it at a maximum of 24°C.

In passing, there was another mistake I made. The gH of the water in London is pretty hard, so, encouraged by the books, I determined to filter my tap water and create Reverse Osmosis (RO) water. There were two problems with this: firstly, RO water tends to make pH low (hence 6.0); and secondly, I didn't then realise I had to replace the lost minerals in RO water with a mineral supplement because, amongst other things, the osmoregulation of fish suffers, and the fish leach salt.

In future I will carry out fishless cycling, and I describe one scenario around fishless cycling elsewhere in this book. Now I know there are arguments for and against fish-in cycling. There are times, I am sure, when it is unavoidable, for instance when a filter breaks down and for some reason you cannot purchase a new filter where you can install your old filter media.

People say another reason is because – if you are buying little eight-year-old Johnny or Sally their first tank – the kids will want to have fish in the tank sooner rather than later: it is quite an ask to expect them to wait five weeks while the filter matures. My response to this is to say that there's a high likelihood that, if you carry out fish-in cycling, little Johnny or Sally will come downstairs one morning and find their prized new fish floating dead on top of the water. Which would you rather? I'm afraid that in my view, fishless cycling is not difficult, and the key ingredients are a drop bottle of ammonia and a degree of patience. Fish-in cycling is arguably very cruel. If you love your fish don't do it, except in extremity.

Beyond this, there is in my view a strong argument that fish-in cycling is in many circumstances in contravention of The Animal Welfare Act 2006 in England and Wales. Section 9 of the Animal Welfare Act places a duty of care on people to ensure they take reasonable steps in all the circumstances to meet the welfare needs of their animals to the extent required by good practice. For these purposes an "animal" is any vertebrate other than a human, and "vertebrate" means any animal of the Sub-phylum Vertebrata of the Phylum Chordata. There is therefore no doubt that the Act covers tropical freshwater fish.

In short, the Act means that those responsible for animals must take positive steps to ensure they care for their animals properly and, in particular, must provide for the five welfare needs, which are, in general terms, the need:

- for a suitable environment
- for a suitable diet
- to be able to exhibit normal behaviour patterns
- to be housed with, or apart, from other animals
- to be protected from pain, suffering, injury and disease.

It seems clear to me that a tank environment in which ammonia and nitrite levels are skyrocketing is not a suitable one for tropical freshwater fish, nor is it good practice. Equally, for reasons discussed in Appendix 2, it is my contention that tropical freshwater fish are sentient and so capable of suffering. Accordingly, there is, as a matter of law at least, a strong incentive to discourage fish-in cycling. As I say, Appendix 2 addresses this in more detail.

Figure 2: Fish purchased for experimental 40-litre tank

Week 2	3 zebra danios
Week 3	5 zebra danios[2]
Week 3	3 zebra danios lost to substandard filter
Week 4	1 zebra danio lost to poor water quality
Week 4	Daily 25% water changes regimen begins
Week 7	Tank cycles
Week 8	2 zebra danios, 2 Amano shrimp, 2 pepper corydoras
Week 9	3 Amano shrimp

When I realised my ammonia and nitrite levels were skyrocketing and I had no option but to get on with my fishless cycling, the cavalry came to the rescue in the form of two buckets, an enormous glass beaker and a bottle of dechlorinator.

---

2   The addition of a further five zebra danios all at once before my tank had cycled was much too aggressive. In retrospect, I should really only have added one or two more. Another mistake.

Every morning at 7 a.m. I would test my water and determine that I immediately needed to do a 20% water change. To begin with I would filter my tap water through an RO filter jug, until eventually I realised this was doing more harm than good (see above, and also Chapter 12).

I would fill a big yellow constructor's bucket with cold tap water and mix it with boiling water from the kettle. Then, after getting a general sense of the temperature by hand, I would throw in a bobbing red glass thermometer and mix and match the water until it was about 26°C. Then I would mix in some dechlorinator and leave the bucket for fifteen minutes.

Then I would stand on a step, fill a glass beaker, and transfer its contents into a second bucket. After repeating this process twenty one times, I would immediately then refill the tank with twenty two glass beakers of dechlorinated water and after that add in 2ml of Dr Tim's First Defense, 5ml of Fluval Biological Enhancer and one squirt of Tropica Premium Nutrition. I would then leave the tank to settle for an hour before taking another test with my API liquid Master Test Kit.

This was gruelling work, and it had to be carried out every day for more than three weeks. Every morning I would wake up and groan as I heaved myself out of bed, reluctant to address the task ahead. But it worked! Suddenly, after just over three weeks, my ammonia and nitrite levels sank down to 0.25ppm and then to 0ppm one after another and I was rewarded with a fully cycled tank.

There was another benefit to this regimen: I was now an expert water changer and had no fear of it. I was well-trained in the need to carry out weekly 20% water changes on a general ongoing basis. I was reminded of George Farmer's recollections in *Aquascaping* around the fact that water changing is a simple reality of life for all discerning aquarists, and I often wonder – with all the aquariums he has at home – if he ever stops water changing.

On the other hand, Diana Walstad, in her book *The Ecology of the Planted Aquarium,* argues that in a well-planted and well-balanced aquarium, in which the plants consume the nitrate as a matter of course, it may only be necessary to change your water about once every six months. This is, I think (from a practical rather than a scientific perspective) an extreme approach; and although my 40-litre tank is very well planted (and I intend my 240-litre tank to be so), I expect that I will still carry out 20% water changes once a week as a precaution.

Finally, on water changing, there are those who argue for and those who argue against RO water. Just be careful: as I have said before, RO water may lower the pH to undesirable levels, and without added minerals it is not good for the fish because without those minerals their osmoregulation can suffer. An RO solution sounds the perfect solution – after all, what can be wrong about adding pure filtered water to your aquarium? – but it has its dangers.

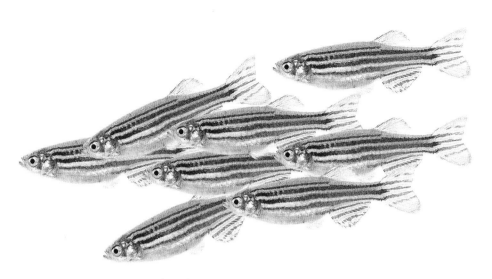

Zebra danios in shoal *(Danio rerio)*

During the period when my ammonia and nitrite levels were sky high (as high as 4ppm at one point, when arguably my fish should have been dead), my Danios were understandably distressed. They rarely gulped for air at the surface, but they lethargically clung to the bottom of the tank and stopped feeding. Every evening I would anxiously inspect them, wondering whether they would exhibit the symptoms of brown gill disease. In brown gill disease, a fish's blood chemistry is compromised by nitrite poisoning, causing its blood and gills to turn brown.

Beyond this, my Danios were unhappy because their shoal had broken down. At one point I had eight *Danio rerio*, but I lost three to my substandard filter and one to poor water conditions. The remaining four were not sufficient in number to form a proper shoal, and they behaved accordingly: a series of four disparate loners, each doing their own thing. The other problem was that I had two females and two males, so, to the extent their lethargy permitted, the males were endlessly pursuing the females, who endlessly had to chase them off, so exhausting themselves.

When my tank cycled and I bought two more female zebra danios, it was amazing how the addition of just two more fish was sufficient to change their behaviour. They immediately began confidently to inhabit all layers of the tank and acted like a coherent whole, shimmering and shuddering and flitting hither and thither in happy synchronicity. I thought about buying another two specimens, bringing the shoal total up to eight, to see if that made coherence even more pronounced; but eventually I decided that discretion was the better part of valour and that I should avoid overstocking my tank.

Even with just six, at last I had a happy shoal. A shoal of zebra danios is a beautiful sight. All those multi-layered dark blue and silver horizontal stripes acting in relative concert as the fish delightedly swim against the filter flow or scrabble for fish flakes at the surface or kiss your fingers in the anticipation of food. It was better than watching Netflix on the television. All those water changes had been worth it!

Call me an old softie, but I would often sit and contemplate the watery biotope my Danios and I had created as I sat in my comfortable old armchair and listened to Camille Saint Saëns' *Aquarium* from his *Carnival of the Animals*. Self-indulgent, perhaps, but what is a cycled, well-stocked and well-planted aquarium for if not to be indulged in?

I was still having a problem with low pH, however. Apart from stopping water changing with RO water (as discussed above), I began to use a Seachem product called Neutral Regulator that promised to buffer pH to 7.0. I was initially a bit dubious about this product, partly because it is best to introduce as few chemicals to a tank as reasonably possible, and partly because it claimed to "detoxify" (rather than "remove") ammonia, and I wanted the ammonia levels to come down naturally without direct chemical intervention.

Seachem products generally have a very good reputation, however, so I put in just under half a teaspoon of Neutral Regulator with each water change. Part of the problem with my low pH level was that my substrate was Tropica Aquarium Soil, which tends to lower pH for a few months, so I felt it was only right to level out this bias with some direct intervention. After the introduction of Neutral Regulator and hard tap water my pH began to climb and after a few doses I managed to get it to stabilise at about 6.8, which was perfect from my perspective. My Danios seemed to love it, too.

Aside from my substandard filter saga, one of the things which slowed down my cycling and disturbed my Danios was a suggestion recommended by one experienced aquarist. After the filter had been maturing for a week or so, the thought was that I should stop feeding the fish for five days and stop water changes for a week and try for what was called a "bacterial bloom", after which my ammonia and nitrite levels would quickly revert to 0ppm.

I tried this approach, but after five days there was no bacterial bloom and as you can imagine my Danios were in great distress because my ammonia and nitrite levels had skyrocketed. I was most distressed myself, as you can imagine, and began to do research into the bacterial bloom concept. The abstract of one paper I found suggested that bacterial blooms would hardly ever occur because nitrifying bacteria grow so slowly that in effect you would be waiting for Godot. Equally, the extreme build up of ammonia and nitrite caused by trying for a bacterial bloom would actually tend to slow the reproduction of nitrifying bacteria down. Accordingly, for all these reasons, let alone the stress caused to the fish by this approach, I would not on current evidence generally recommend trying for a bacterial bloom.

One morning I woke up to find my Danios swimming mid-level. I tested urgently. The ammonia came in at 0.50ppm, the nitrite at 2ppm. This was progress. I tested again next morning. The ammonia came in a 0ppm, the nitrite at 1ppm. That night I tested again. The ammonia and nitrite both came in at 0ppm. This was a typical pattern for the endgame for a cycling tank. The ammonia-eating *Nitrosomonas* bacteria multiply slightly faster than the nitrite-eating *Nitrobacter* bacteria[3].

I tested my nitrate to check that the *Nitrobacter* bacteria were doing their job. The nitrate came in at 30ppm. I had triumphed! My tank was fully cycled. For the first day in over three weeks I wrote in my aquarist's notebook that I would not be doing a water change that day – although my nitrate level was quite high[4], my tank was heavily planted and I had confidence that my thriving plants would soon cycle the nitrate.

Now my mind turned to stocking up my tank. I had been told by one experienced aquarist to wait a week after the tank had cycled to let it settle before considering getting more stock, and after my horrendous experience I was not going to push things.

Nevertheless, precisely one week after my tank had cycled, I found myself stomping the pavement towards the fish store. In I went. It's always a pleasure visiting a fish store. When you enter you are assaulted by darkness and a rather humid sensation together with an almost musty smell of water – it's not musty at all of course, but that's the way it feels. Then you focus in on the banks of tanks lining the walls and stacked four or five tanks high. Full of all types of fish, from neon and cardinal tetras to discus fish (*Symphysodon*). Seemingly an endless pescatarian plethora. If only I could buy them all and bring them all home to plenish my tank – impossible of course. But I had entered an Aladdin's cave of ichthyological wonder.

The owner knew me by sight, and I told him what had happened to my tank and that I wanted to make a modest purchase of two female zebra danios, two pepper Corydoras catfish and three Amano shrimp. The owner tested my water (a sample of which I had brought to the store in a test tube) and complimented me on its excellent quality. That made me preen, I can tell you, but I knew it had been hard-earned – and I told him so!

---

3   Some microbiologists argue that *Nitrosomonas* and *Nitrobacter* bacteria are not the correct bacteria to be found in a typical aquarium because they tend to be found in sewage and water treatment systems where ammonia and nitrite levels are much higher. Despite this, for the purposes of this book I shall describe the relevant nitrifying bacteria as *Nitrosomonas* and *Nitrobacter* because this appears to remain the most prevalent view.
4   Although the base nitrate level for my tap water is 20ppm in any event.

He then had no hesitation in preparing a plastic bag and caught up the relevant fish deftly in a net before placing them gently in the bag. It never ceases to amaze me how the owners of fish stores can so competently wield a net – it puts my clumsy efforts to shame. Finally, I bought a bright green moss ball to keep the Amano shrimp happy.

I gingerly walked home, barely daring to walk on the cracks in the pavement just in case my body overly vibrated and I upset the fish. Then I opened the lid of my tank and floated the plastic bag on top for twenty minutes to equalise the temperature. I cut open the top of the bag with scissors and poured in 20ml of tank water every five minutes for another twenty minutes to get the fish and shrimp used to the water quality in the tank, otherwise they might have been shocked. Finally, with a shudder of joy, I poured the fish and shrimp into the tank.

While this was going on my four tank zebra danios were crowding round the bag, as if inquisitive to know what was going on. As soon as my two new Danios were released, they joined the group, and they immediately began shoaling as I described above.

My 40 litre tank after cycling

At the same time my Amano shrimp began feasting on the algae on top of the filter. I observed them all day, as they boldly went about their business in plain view. I thought that every day would be like this, but I was wrong. The next morning my shrimp were nowhere to be seen, and they afforded me only cursory glimpses every other day or so from then on in. Someone told me that adjusting to the new tank may have incited them to shed their exoskeleton and they were hiding while their new coat hardened. One morning I peered in the tank to see a dead Amano shrimp on the substrate. I picked it up sadly with a pair of long tweezers, only to discover it was just a shed exoskeleton, and I breathed a huge sigh of relief.

The catfish were another matter. They furtively took to ground immediately, and I didn't see sight or sound of the little blighters for two days. This worried me immensely, not least because I didn't want feeding them to upset the water quality in the tank. The problem was I was leaving out catfish pellets and algae wafers for the catfish, but they didn't seem the least bit interested. I had been told that they often feed at night, so I left the food out for them overnight, although my Danios seemed much more interested in it than my corys.

Amano shrimp *(Caridina multidentate)*

On the third morning I woke up and all the remains of the algae wafers had gone. Then I saw one cory scouring a rock for algae; and soon I saw the second playfully riding the flow from the filter backwards and forwards as if riding the corkscrew at the funfair. I breathed another sigh of relief. My corys were going to be fine; and more than that, they were going to be real little characters. Eventually they learned where on the substrate I drop their catfish pellets, and they make a beeline for that spot every evening.

Feeding was a problem at this point because I had a tendency to overfeed (see also Chapter 12). I fed my Danios three tiny pinches of fish flakes three times a day. They went crazy, circling and jumping and grasping for food – all six of them. In the early stages I caught the remnants of their meal that were floating on the surface with a net to stop detritus sinking to the bottom of the tank. But soon I stopped doing this. First, as my Danio shoal became more adventurous, so every time I skimmed the surface with a net, I would catch one or two Danios in it, and I didn't want to damage them by frequent netting. Equally, I figured that at least some food had to fall to the bottom to keep the corys and Amano shrimp well-served.

Every three days or so I would give my fish a treat by feeding them some daphnia that I had bought frozen from the fish store. I always get a little alarmed when this happens, because the daphnia tends to fall to the bottom or get caught in the fronds of plants in clumps. So it's critical to stir the daphnia up. But when you do that, it goes everywhere. The day after a daphnia feed, I always have my heart in my mouth in trepidation just in case my ammonia test spikes, but to date that has never happened. I suppose that is the benefit of having two hungry catfish and three voracious Amano shrimp, not to mention a well-cycled filter.

The bottom line is the fish go wild for daphnia. I suppose it's the ichthyological equivalent of going to a two-star Michelin restaurant. So, despite my trepidations, I certainly won't start denying them that privilege. In any event, watching them dart hither and thither in delight as they lurch for every last morsel is a thrill to behold.

I finally figured out how to feed my tank daphnia in a controlled manner. I would defrost a daphnia cube in the microwave's low setting, and then separate out about a third of the cube. I would take that third and sit it into a small glass full of tank water, and then pour the contents into the tank. This works a treat, but it is still quite messy.

After another week of all this I was faced with a fresh dilemma. I had originally intended for a tank of eight zebra danios, two pepper corys and five Amano shrimp. On a level, my Danios would love an even bigger shoal. But my tank was

Leopard corydoras *(Corydoras leopardus)*

so heavily planted there was not that much room for free swimming space, and the tank looked pretty crowded with just six Danios.

I did a quick stocking density calculation, based on the internal filter ratio of 1.2 cm of fish to one litre of tank water. Adult zebra danios can grow to 5 cm, while adult pepper corys can grow up to about the same. So that comes to 36 litres. I could just about squeeze two more Danios into my tank, but I came to the conclusion I would stick with six, since the shoal on the whole seemed perfectly happy. And it seemed to me I now had a happy and well-balanced tank.

All of this only confirmed what I already knew from my youth: I loved keeping fish. I loved the technical aspects, the nod to chemistry and biology and zoology. I loved the obsession with equipment and the latest fad; I loved the humid fug of the fish stores and their dark secretive recesses that accommodated every conceivable species of tropical fish; I loved the camaraderie of hobbyists' forums such as the UK Aquatic Plant Society. But most of all, I loved creating – Aquascaping – a little enclosed world of its own with plants and rocks and soil and fish all sustained by a state-of-the-art internal filter containing a colony of seemingly magical nitrifying bacteria. And within that world existed a shoal of zebra danios and pepper corys whose antics make the heart glow, but who rely on you for everything. The whole thing was a seemingly miraculous synthesis of science, art and nature.

Already my corys had little personalities of their own – you expect that in corys – but my Danios equally had their personalities. The two that stood out most for me were the largest female, whom I called "The Matriarch", and the smallest male, whom I called "The Little Warrior". He earned that title because he had been one of the Danios that had got themselves caught in the substandard filter. But I had got to him in time, and he had somehow survived. In any event, these two had been through thick and thin with me, because they had inadvertently formed part of my "suicide squad", and they had braved out the adverse water conditions when the ammonia and nitrite were each spiking at 4ppm.

In a word, I was in love. The trouble was, this was extremely inconvenient. How long does a zebra danio live? About four years, they say, with a fair wind[5]. But there's not always a fair wind, and there is always the possibility of an early demise. I got used to the fact that fish can easily die early thanks to my substandard filter. I had chosen zebra danios because I knew they were hardy. But, notwithstanding The Little Warrior, two Danios died in the filter, and a third survived the ordeal but had his pectoral fins ripped off in the process. After watching him writhing at the bottom of the tank for an hour just to make sure there was no chance of a miraculous recovery, I determined I had to put him to sleep on welfare grounds. I sadly plucked him from the substrate and reluctantly dropped him into a glass

---

5   A cory can live as long as ten years, however.

of aquarium water infused with Clove Oil[6], which did the job nicely. Of course, I observed him carefully for half an hour, making sure there were no gill movements or eye rolls, etc (in accordance with RSPCA advice) to ensure he was dead before sealing him in a plastic bag and disposing of him in the bin.

Make no mistake: if you keep fish, even with the best of intentions, now and again they will die. That's the risk you take when you risk love. Four years is all you get – with a cory maybe much more – but what a four years. When I wake up every morning, turn on the light, gaze into the little special integrated world I have created and see my Danios crowing at the surface urgently looking for food, I realise that those moments of occasional heartache when you must bag a dead fish and throw it in the bin – the modern and more responsible equivalent of flushing it down the loo – are more than offset by the joy of the fish tank.

And if that weren't enough consolation, look at it this way. Danios in the wild get trampled underfoot in rice paddies or eaten by predators such as herons, kingfishers and other fish. What's the average life expectancy of a zebra danio in the wild, I wonder? So, it is quite possible that for a Danio to live in a fish tank is for it to have won first prize in the ichthyological lottery of life.

For myself, I won't stop buying tickets!

---

6   Dosage 400mg per litre of water, introduced in increments over a five-minute period.

5

The invocation of an obsession and tropical freshwater fish in art and literature

A dark gallery. Black rubber tiles on the floor that make your shoes squeak. A winding trail of seemingly endless palaeontological exhibits lit up through the darkness by bright white spotlights. The Ulster Museum, 1974. Round a corner from an ammonite fossil sits a long exhibit a bit like a fish tank. In it lies a long bulbous fish with a near terminal mouth and strange-looking scales. On the tank are emblazoned the words:

"The Coelacanth – the Living Fossil"

I visited the Ulster Museum nearly every Sunday in those days because our next door neighbour, who was a curator, used to bring me to keep me out of mischief. And every Sunday I would make a beeline for the coelacanth exhibit.

What is a coelacanth? Well, it's a prehistoric fish that was discovered in the 19th century in the fossil record and was thought to be long extinct until the netting of a live one in 1938. Wikipedia puts it like this:

> "The earliest fossils of coelacanths were discovered in the 19th century. Coelacanths, which are related to lungfishes and tetrapods, were believed to have become extinct at the end of the Cretaceous period. More closely related to tetrapods than to the ray-finned fish, coelacanths were considered transitional species between fish and tetrapods. On 23 December 1938, the first *Latimeria* specimen was found off the east coast of South Africa, off the Chalumna River (now Tyolomnqa) … Its discovery 66 million years after its supposed extinction makes the coelacanth the best-known example of a Lazarus taxon, an evolutionary line that seems to have disappeared from the fossil record only to reappear much later."

Every Sunday I would obsessively take in all the observable details of this fish. Its eyes, its mouth, its primitive armoured scales. It was a massive beast. Coelacanths can grow up to two metres and weigh up to 90 kg. They can live up to sixty years old. I was mesmerised at this living link back to the dinosaurs. Wikipedia again:

> "[Coelacanths] are nocturnal piscivorous drift-hunters. The body is covered in cosmoid scales that act as armor. Coelacanths have eight fins – 2 dorsal fins, 2 pectoral fins, 2 pelvic fins, 1 anal fin and 1 caudal fin. The tail is very nearly equally proportioned and is split by a terminal tuft of fin rays that make up its caudal lobe. The eyes of the coelacanth are very large, while the mouth is very small. The eye is acclimatized to seeing in poor light by rods that absorb mostly short wavelengths…"

Everything about the coelacanth oozed mystery and mystique. It's my first recollection of falling in love with a fish – even a dead Lazarus Taxon preserved in a tank.

Apart from my community tank as a teenager, my youth and young adulthood seemed to be a progression of aquariums around the globe. My parents would take us on driving holidays throughout Britain, during which I would be treated to the London Zoo and its Aquarium, Chester Zoo and its Aquarium[7], and of course Belfast Zoo. Later in life, when visiting my in-laws near Hull, I would frequent The Deep, a magnificent contemporary aquarium based nearby. I always found visits to zoo aquariums the most magical of experiences. In I would go, into the dark, cool, dank, humid aquarium house, leaving the bright glare of the sunshine and the monkeys, lions, penguins and gorillas outside. Inside it would be almost silent, a world away from the bothersome squawking and screeching of the main exhibits. It was less crowded, too – a lot of people seemed to pass the aquarium by, considering it less exciting than the rhino house or the giraffe enclosure. Once inside, as my eyes adjusted, I then focussed in on a miasma of joy as tank upon tank of colourful fish assaulted me. And of course, there were all those wonderful written scientific explanations at the side of the tank.

There were more joyous aquarium experiences as life went on. When I moved to London I would visit the London Aquarium. When I started going out with my then girlfriend, now wife, who lived in Hamburg and had friends in Frankfurt, there was the Frankfurt Zoo Aquarium. And then of course there was The Deep – which became especially beloved by my children too, when they were younger.

My favourite aquarium of all around this time was a rather understated one. When in Belfast I would often drive through County Down along the west coast of Strangford Lough and take the little car ferry across the mouth of the Lough from Strangford to Portaferry. I would park up and have a drink in the lovely

---

7   Fortuitously, my wife is from Cheshire, so I have also visited Chester Zoo Aquarium numerous times in adulthood.

Aquarium

aus dem "Karneval der Tiere"

Camille Saint-Saëns
Arr.: Patrick Egge

Transcript of the commencement of 'Aquarium' from 'The Carnival of the Animals', by Camille Saint-Saëns (1886)

Portaferry Hotel on the waterfront before ambling down behind the ruins of the castle. There, tucked away and obscured from easy view, sat a little gem – the Portaferry Aquarium. It wasn't very big, and had more than its fair share of marine exhibits, as you can imagine, but it was beautiful and well-maintained. I whiled many an afternoon away there; and, when my community tank had long gone, my visits to Portaferry did just enough to keep the aquarist's spark going in my heart – a sort of ichthyological pilot light. It was waiting. For re-ignition.

Another aspect of my life that kept my pilot light going around this time was my father. He was the strong, silent type and whenever I visited home we would watch nature documentaries together as we communed in the half-dark. It didn't matter what the programmes were about: the spawning regimen of salmon, coral reefs, the hunting behaviour of sharks – all was up for grabs. And although very few of these programmes were about tropical freshwater fish in themselves, they

Wucai fish jar from British Museum (1567–1572)

maintained my interest in zoology and conservation. For thirty years my love for tropical freshwater fish was kept on the back burner. But because of all these positive influences, it was never extinguished.

It's not just me who has a love of aquariums and tropical freshwater fish. Many artists and writers of all hues have recorded their love of fish in art. I have already mentioned Camille Saint-Saëns' celebrated musical work *The Carnival of the Animals*, which includes a section entitled *Aquarium*. From the very first bars of this work, he evokes a watery world where fish blow bubbles and sink from the surface to the substrate. The descending glissando chords create an image of a mysterious descent into an ephemeral world upon which mankind can only gaze, forbidden from participating. On many occasions I have gazed lovingly at my fish tank while playing this music and dreaming of the joy of beautifully interacting, gaudily coloured tropical fish. I urge anyone the vaguest bit interested in music or aquariums to search up and stream *Aquarium* while observing their fish tank with a glass of wine.

And it's not just music. The Chinese and Japanese love their fish, especially goldfish, which they regard as symbols of wealth and prosperity. This is partly because the Chinese word for "fish" also translates as "abundance". Goldfish and Corydoras feature as painting beneath the glaze of *wucai* fish jars. Wikipedia describes *wucai* porcelain as follows: "*Wucai*, (五彩 "Five colours", "Wuts'ai" in Wade-Giles) is a style of decorating white Chinese porcelain in a limited range of colours. It normally uses underglaze cobalt blue for the design outline and some parts of the images, and overglaze enamels in red, green, and yellow for the rest of the designs."

Some *wucai* jars are extremely old, dating from the Ming Dynasty. An example of a prestigious *wucai* fish jar in the British Museum is shown here (see above).

Painting, too, sees its fair share of representations of tropical freshwater fish. A painting called *Goldfish* (see next page), by well-known Chinese-French artist Sanyu (1895–1966), was sold by Christies in December 2020 for HK$1,170,000. This beautiful painting, which evokes the poignancy of a columnar nano tank,

'Goldfish', by Sanyu (1895–1966)

captures the flailing movement of the fish as they adjust to the limitations of their world. Another contemporary painter, American James Prosek, captures a canny depiction of shoaling fish (see below). An abstract by him of a fish out of water was exhibited at the Royal Academy in 2019.

Early depictions of fish in paintings seem to have revolved around religious themes such as the miraculous catch or the feeding of the five thousand, although in the 17th century a tradition of fish-orientated still life emerged from the Dutch School. One example is *Still Life of Fish* by Abraham van Beyeren (circa 1655), shown on the next page. More recently, religious paintings of fish have become more abstract and symbolic. See *Purposeful Ichthus* and *Scripture Fish* by J. Vincent Scarpace (1971–), as shown on the following page. These abstract depictions seem to me to be extremely poetic and powerful. It's not surprising, therefore, that a number of poignant poems about aquariums have been composed. Perhaps one of the most famous of these is, like Sanyu's painting above, about goldfish: *Goldfish* by Valerie Worth ...

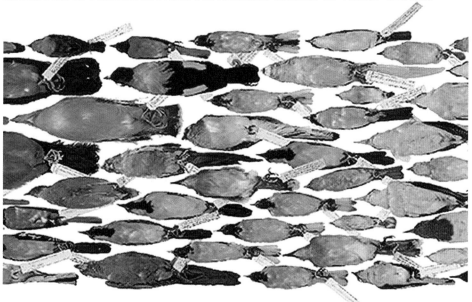

'Fish', by James Prosek (Circa 2019)

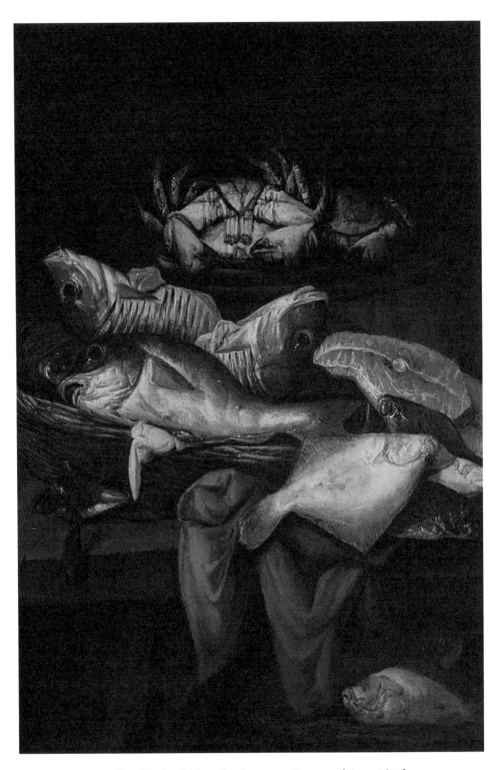

'Still Life of Fish', by Abraham van Beyeren (circa 1655)

'Purposeful Ichthus by Two', by J. Vincent Scarpace (1971–)

'Scripture Fish', by J. Vincent Scarpace (1971–)

Goldfish by Valerie Worth

Goldfish
Flash
Gold and silver scales;
They flick and slip away ... under green weed
But round brown snails
Stick
To the glass
And stay

This effective poem gracefully describes the frustration all of us aquarists feel when the fish we are observing craftily slinks behind the nearest clump of *Cabomba*. It contrasts powerfully with the following poem by Kim Addonizio, who deftly describes every aquarist's fear when they open up the lid of the tank, especially if they are keeping hatchet fish (*Gasteropelecus sternicla*) or their ilk:

Aquarium
by Kim Addonizio

THE FISH are drifting calmly in their tank
between the green reeds, lit by a white glow
that passes for the sun. Blindly, the blank
glass that holds them in displays their slow
progress from end to end, familiar rocks
set into the gravel, murmuring rows
of filters, a universe the flying fox
and glass cats, Congo tetras, bristle-nose
pleocostemus all take for granted. Yet
the platys, gold and red, persist in leaping
occasionally, as if they can't quite let
alone a possibility—of wings,
maybe, once they reach the air? They die
on the rug. We find them there, eyes open in surprise.

Finally, a very recent poem by D.W. Rodgers describes the power struggles within a cichlid tank. It seems to me to be written in very loose form, almost conversational, as if the poet were gently showing the reader around his tank and frankly expressing all his worst fears for his husbandry of these most challenging of tropical freshwater fish.

Aquarium
by D.W. Rodgers

The cichlids patrol their 48"x18"x18" tank and
though this country has been officially metric since
April Fool's day, 1975, I still measure fish and tanks
in inches, feet, ounces, pounds and gallons.
A mix of African cichlids, from lakes Victoria and
Tanganyika, but tanks are the only world they've known.
Cichlids are of interest to me because of their diversity,
they're the fish equivalent of Galapagos finches.
But I really keep them because their bright colours and
constant motion especially at feeding time provides
a brief respite from the humdrum.

Each species more or less keeps to themselves,
establishing ever shifting territories in the
nooks and crannies of the rock wall I built,
that runs through the middle of the tank.
There is a balance of density and species,
which I never quite manage to maintain and
as they mature, intra and interspecific aggression
becomes a factor and every so often, I'll find
a beat-up loser floating at the top of the tank.
But other times they breed successfully and
if I separate the mouthbrooding female early
enough, I can raise another generation of fry.

Perhaps the most famous poem coincidentally to involve freshwater fish is by Thomas Gray (1716–1771). His "Ode on the Death of a Favourite Cat Drowned in a Tub of Goldfishes" is a deliberately satirical work that exaggerates his cat's death. Along with "Elegy Written in a Country Churchyard", it is one of Gray's most famous poems. This poem will remind all fishkeepers with cats (including me) of the hazards of cats with regards to fish tanks – and, ironically, that the hazards flow both ways.

Ode on the Death of a Favourite Cat
Drowned in a Tub of Goldfishes
by Thomas Gray

'Twas on a lofty vase's side,
Where China's gayest art had dyed
The azure flowers that blow;
Demurest of the tabby kind,
The pensive Selima, reclined,
Gazed on the lake below.

Her conscious tail her joy declared;
The fair round face, the snowy beard,
The velvet of her paws,
Her coat, that with the tortoise vies,
Her ears of jet, and emerald eyes,
She saw; and purred applause.

Still had she gazed; but 'midst the tide
Two angel forms were seen to glide,
The genii of the stream;
Their scaly armour's Tyrian hue
Through richest purple to the view
Betrayed a golden gleam.

The hapless nymph with wonder saw;
A whisker first and then a claw,
With many an ardent wish, She
stretched in vain to reach the prize.
What female heart can gold despise?
What cat's averse to fish?

Presumptuous maid! with looks intent
Again she stretch'd, again she bent,
Nor knew the gulf between.
(Malignant Fate sat by, and smiled)
The slippery verge her feet beguiled,
She tumbled headlong in.

Eight times emerging from the flood
She mewed to every watery god,
Some speedy aid to send.
No dolphin came, no Nereid stirred;
Nor cruel Tom, nor Susan heard;
A Favourite has no friend!

From hence, ye beauties, undeceived,
Know, one false step is ne'er retrieved,
And be with caution bold.
Not all that tempts your wandering eyes
And heedless hearts, is lawful prize;
Nor all that glisters, gold.

Finally, on poetry, one of the most famous relatively contemporary poems about fish is "Fish" by D.H. Lawrence. As might be expected, the poem deserves a careful reading, but it is too long to set out here in its entirety. There follows, however, one brief excerpt, where Lawrence captures the iconic mysterious beauty of fish:

Fishes,

With their gold, red eyes, and green-pure gleam, and under-gold,

And their pre-world loneliness,

And more-than-lovelessness.

And white meat;

They move in other circles.

On a more literary theme, it is always prudent to start with William Shakespeare. Perhaps not surprisingly, there do not seem to be any quotes from Shakespeare about tropical freshwater fish or aquariums. There are, however, a number of quotes about where fish sit in the pecking order of things, particularly when it comes to fishing.

Perhaps the most famous fish quote in Shakespeare comes from *Hamlet*: "A man may fish with the worm that hath eat of a king, and eat of the fish that have fed of that worm." On a similar theme, from *Pericles, Prince of Tyre*: "Fishes live in the sea, as men do a-land; the great ones eat up the little ones." This is an abbreviated quote. The full transcription is as follows:

> **Third Fisherman:** Nay, master, said not I as much when I
> saw the porpus how he bounced and tumbled? they say
> they're half fish, half flesh: a plague on them,
> they ne'er come but I look to be washed. Master, I
> marvel how the fishes live in the sea.

> **First Fisherman:** Why, as men do a-land; the great ones
> eat up the little ones: I can compare our rich misers to
> nothing so fitly as to a whale; a' plays and
> tumbles, driving the poor fry before him, and at
> last devours them all at a mouthful: such whales
> have I heard on o' the land, who never leave gaping
> till they've swallowed the whole parish, church,
> steeple, bells, and all.

Pericles [Aside]: A pretty moral.

From *The Comedy of Errors* comes another reference: "Ay, when fowls have no feathers and fish have no fin." The full transcription:

> **Dromio of Ephesus:** Here's too much "out upon thee!" I pray thee, let me in.
>
> **Dromio of Syracuse:** (within) Ay, when fowls have no feathers and fish have no fin.
>
> **Antipholus of Ephesus:** Well, I'll break in. Go, borrow me a crow.
>
> **Dromio of Ephesus:** A crow without a feather? Master, mean you so? For a fish without a fin, there's a fowl without a feather – (to Dromio of Syracuse) If a crow help us in, sirrah, we'll pluck a crow together.

John Ruskin continued the tradition when in *The Two Paths* (1859) he stated that: "No human being, however great or powerful, was ever as free as a fish", while Andre Gide in his *Journals* (May, 1930) observed that: "Fish die belly-upward and rise to the surface. It is their way of falling." A sad but inevitable moment for any fishkeeper, because at the end of the day to keep fish and fall in love with them is to court ephemera.

One literary proverb from Ancient Babylon I love because, although it is intended to refer to bait fishing, I imagine that it reflects God's view of aquarium fishkeeping (it was often quoted by Herbert Hoover): "The gods do not deduct from man's allotted span the hours spent in fishing."

There are a few contemporary novels that have aquariums as a focal point. One in particular is *Aquarium* by David Vann. Goodreads offers the following synopsis:

> "Twelve-year-old Caitlin lives alone with her mother—a docker at the local container port—in subsidized housing next to an airport in Seattle. Each day, while she waits to be picked up after school, Caitlin visits the local aquarium to study the fish. Gazing at the creatures within the watery depths, Caitlin accesses a shimmering universe beyond her own. When she befriends an old man at the tanks one day, who seems as enamored of the fish as she, Caitlin cracks open a dark family secret and propels her once-blissful relationship with her mother toward a precipice of terrifying consequence.
>
> In crystalline, chiseled yet graceful prose, *Aquarium* takes us into the heart of a brave young girl whose longing for love and capacity for forgiveness transforms the damaged people around her."

There is one particularly poignant description of a dream in an aquarium. I suspect all aquarists have had a moment like this when they imagine sinking to the bottom of a tank they curate:

"When I went to sleep each night, I imagined myself at the bottom, thousands of feet down, the weight of all that water but I was gliding just above ground, something like a manta ray, flying soundless and weightless over endless plains that fell away into deep canyons of darker black and then rose up in spires and new plateaus, and I could be anywhere in this world, off Mexico or Guam or under the Arctic or all the way to Africa, all in the one element, all home, shadows on all sides of me gliding also, great wings without sound or sight but felt and known."

Otherwise, most of the relevant quotations in Vann's book seem rather opaque, referring to fish and aquariums as metaphors for some deep aspect of human psychology:

"Each one a little bit different but following some blueprint somewhere. As if each of us might have a blueprint. As if somewhere there's the shape of my life, and I had the chance to choose a few variations, but not far from the pattern.

Origins... They don't explain us, you know. They never do. Each of us is our own piece of work.

This is what I've always loved about a city, all the worlds hidden away inside, largest of aquariums.

The entire legacy of humanity will be only one thing, a line of red goop in the paleo-oceanographic record, a time of no calcium carbonate shells that will stretch on for several million years. The sadness of our stupidity is overwhelming."

Despite these scattered and occasional gems, given the beauty of a well-hardscaped, well-planted and well-maintained Aquascape, it is perhaps extremely surprising there are not more effusive descriptions and depictions of aquariums in art and literature. When, for instance, I started my research into this chapter, my first port of call was Gerald Durrell. If anyone would have a contemporary description of an aquarium it would surely be him. But I was to be disappointed.

Equally, I researched Charles Dickens from this perspective, but all I could find was a reference to "Mr Guppy" in *Bleak House*, which was serialised in 1852–53. In the context of tropical fish, however, the first mention of guppies was probably in a zoological work of 1859, in which they were named after a zoologist called Guppy, so it seems unlikely there is any fish-related connection with *Bleak House* unless the Mr Guppy in the novel is based upon that zoologist or one of his ancestors.

Mr Guppy has been described (on the LitCharts website) as: "a young clerk in Mr Kenge's office. An ambitious, self-interested man and a social climber, Mr Guppy cares a great deal about his appearance and reputation and is primarily interested in advancing his social status. Throughout the novel, he serves as a figure of ridicule and a comic relief character."

Does this description evoke the personality of your average guppy fish? Perhaps Mr Guppy the zoologist fits the bill? Whatever, only guppy enthusiasts are qualified to come to a view. Moreover, I was surprised at how unimaginative the titles for some of these works of art were: "Fish", "Goldfish", "Aquarium". How about "Glistening Sheen" or "Multicoloured Scales in Flight" or some such? Anything but the bland "Aquarium."

I suppose the most contemporaneous expositions of visual art around nature are to be found in natural history documentaries, especially the "greats" such as *Life on Earth*, *Living Planet* and *Planet Earth*. These are tours de force, and the photography and narration are sublime. But not much of these programmes concentrates on tropical freshwater fish. Even *Blue Planet* is given over almost exclusively to marine species. Nevertheless, fish generally feature prominently in these documentaries. Most recently, *Seaspiracy*, a Netflix documentary, exposes the vagaries of the marine fishing trade and the problems with seaborne plastics. Despite the fact I would argue the programme seeks to glorify the producer-narrator as much as offer an honest account of the situation, it is still a powerful programme and potentially a landmark of its genre.

Perhaps there is scope for a mini-series of nature documentaries about tropical freshwater fish, their breeding and conservation, possibly divided up into those in lentic, lotic and wetland environments.

So there is a great lacuna. It is perhaps the duty of fishkeepers everywhere to persuade the artistic and literary community of the validity of aquariums and Aquascapes as an art form. Only then perhaps will aquariums take their proper place as part of the essential backdrop of artistic endeavour. Aquariums can be art, and art can reflect aquariums. Let it be so.

Finally in this analysis, let us not forget how freshwater fish have inspired seemingly endless generations of fishkeepers, from the Ancient Sumerians, to the early Chinese, to the Romans, to the more recent Victorian naturalists. A general timeline of the aquarium in history is set out at Appendix 6.

This appendix suggests that the origins of fishkeeping were motivated by self-interested aquaculture through the construction of fishponds to house fish for eating. Gradually, however, this activity developed into a parallel interest in keeping and breeding fish for purely ornamental purposes. Although aquacultural fishkeeping seems to have originated with the Mesopotamians, it emerged ornamentally through the Chinese and the Romans to influence the ponds and pleasure gardens of many cultures, including in India and the Muslim world.

Never forget that we aquarists are the inheritors and custodians of the arts of the ancient fishkeepers. We must guard our treasures well!

The coelacanth *(Coelacanthiformes)*

6

Tropical freshwater fish and conservation

Let's face it, keeping tropical fish is good for the environment. It helps to conserve global fish stocks, raises awareness of conservation issues and highlights the relative fragility of ecosystems.

There are potential adverse consequences, too. Where fish are harvested for tropical tanks from the wild, there is a risk that the stocks in nature might become severely depleted and the habitats in which the fish live damaged or destroyed. It is therefore essential that tropical freshwater aquarists take a responsible attitude and promote and support captive breeding programmes where they can.

The necessity for aquarists' awareness of species depletion and habitat loss reflects the current concern about the reduction in biodiversity across our planet.

The *Global Biodiversity Outlook (5) Report 2020* states that:

"Humanity stands at a crossroads with regard to the legacy it leaves to future generations. Biodiversity is declining at an unprecedented rate, and the pressures driving this decline are intensifying. None of the *Aichi Biodiversity Targets* will be fully met, in turn threatening the achievement of the Sustainable Development Goals and undermining efforts to address climate change. The COVID-19 pandemic has further highlighted the importance of the relationship between people and nature, and it reminds us all of the profound consequences to our own well-being and survival that can result from continued biodiversity loss and the degradation of ecosystems. Nevertheless, reports provided by the world's governments, as well as other sources of evidence, reveal examples of progress which, if scaled up, could support the transformative changes necessary to achieve the 2050 vision of living in harmony with nature. A number of transitions pointing the way to the type of changes required are already in evidence, albeit in limited areas of activity. Examining how such incipient transitions can be replicated and built on, will be critical to using the short window available to make the collective vision of living in harmony with nature a reality."

In 2020 the nineteen *Aichi Biodiversity Targets* had not been met. These are a number of empirical measurements designed to determine the extent to which humanity is taking biodiversity seriously. The first Target for instance, is: "By 2020, at the latest, people are aware of the values of biodiversity and the steps they can take to conserve and use it sustainably."

The Amazon River

Target 5 is: "By 2020, the rate of loss of all natural habitats, including forests, is at least halved and where feasible brought close to zero, and degradation and fragmentation is significantly reduced." Likewise, Target 6 is: "By 2020 all fish and invertebrate stocks and aquatic plants are managed and harvested sustainably, legally and applying ecosystem based approaches, so that overfishing is avoided, recovery plans and measures are in place for all depleted species, fisheries have no significant adverse impacts on threatened species and vulnerable ecosystems and the impacts of fisheries on stocks, species and ecosystems are within safe ecological limits."

This would to my mind include harvesting tropical freshwater fish for the aquarium trade. Target 11 is important for aquarists, and argues strongly for the avoidance of stocking fish for aquariums from the wild where possible: "By 2020, at least 17% of terrestrial and inland water areas and 10% of coastal and marine areas, especially areas of particular importance for biodiversity and ecosystem services, are conserved through effectively and equitably managed, ecologically representative and well-connected systems of protected areas and other effective area-based conservation measures, and integrated into the wider landscape and seascape."

The report proposes a sustainable freshwater transition: an integrated approach guaranteeing the water flows required by nature and people, improving water quality, protecting critical habitats, controlling invasive species and safeguarding connectivity to allow the recovery of freshwater systems from mountains to coasts. This transition recognizes the importance of biodiversity in maintaining the multiple roles of freshwater ecosystems to support human societies and natural processes, including linkages with terrestrial, coastal and marine environments.

Of course, how this will be achieved is up to us. The bottom line is that globally biodiversity is shrinking, and aquarists must pay their responsible part in reversing that trend.

In this context, WWF concludes that habitat loss is probably the greatest threat to the variety of life on this planet today. So habitat loss... "is identified as a main threat to 85% of all species described in the International Union for Conservation's (IUCN) Red List (those species officially classified as *Threatened* and *Endangered*). Increasing food production is a major agent for the conversion of natural habitat into agricultural land." WWF further states that:

> "Forest loss and degradation is mostly caused by the expansion of agricultural land, intensive harvesting of timber, wood for fuel and other forest products, as well as overgrazing.

> The net loss in global forest area during the 1990s was about 94 million ha (equivalent to 2.4% of total forests). It is estimated that in the 1990s, almost 70% of deforested areas were converted to agricultural land.

> Around half of the world's original forests have disappeared, and they are still being removed at a rate 10x higher than any possible level of regrowth. As tropical forests contain at least half the Earth's species, the clearance of some 17 million hectares each year is a dramatic loss. Human impact on terrestrial and marine natural resources results in marine and coastal degradation. Population growth, urbanization, industrialization and tourism are all factors."

It's obvious from all this that the habitats which harbour our beloved tropical freshwater fish are shrinking fast. For a salutary lesson in this regard, just look at Brazil. Brazil is fundamental to fishkeepers, because it hosts most of the Amazon rainforest and of course the Amazon itself. Who can say how many species of tropical freshwater fish emanate from Brazil, including, as a start, Tetras and Corydoras?

And yet this ecosystem is being destroyed at an alarming rate, encouraging deforestation, erosion and pollution. An early draft of an article I wrote on this subject, scheduled for publication in the *Irish Times* in Summer 2021 in advance of COP26 in Glasgow, is set out at Appendix 3. It explores the subject in more detail. However, there follows an excerpt from that piece:

> "The Amazon is located mostly in Brazil and currently comprises about six million square kilometers of rainforest. It is currently being cut down at the rate of about 200,000 acres a day.
>
> The effect this will have on biodiversity is obvious, but a big problem in terms of climate change is that trees store CO_2 of which the Amazon is estimated to capture about 400 billion tons. The release of this will have an important effect on greenhouse gasses and so the ability of the world to keep global mean temperature rise below 2°C, ideally to 1.5°C as envisioned by Paris.
>
> There are other implications. There will almost certainly be a detrimental effect on weather systems, and we have already seen forest fires raging. There will be implications on soil erosion and question-marks over the long-term viability of cleared farmland."

Equally, according to AZ Central's website, the Amazon is becoming increasingly polluted:

> "While the Amazon River is the world's second-longest – behind the Nile – it is the largest in terms of volume, according to National Geographic's website. The Amazon River contains 20% of the fresh water on Earth and its freshwater systems contain minerals that are important to fertilising land in the rainforest. Water pollution is worsening in the Amazon as a result of extensive logging in the rainforest. Areas that were once thick with trees have been converted into open plains, resulting in forest flooding. Gold mining is leading to mercury pollution and dams that are being built in the river basin may alter the flow of water in the river."

As if habitat loss was not bad enough, it exacerbates and is compounded by species loss. Biologists estimate there are between five and fifteen million species of plants, animals, and micro-organisms existing on Earth today, of which only about 1.5 million have so far been described and named. The estimated total includes around 300,000 plant species, between four and eight million insects, and about 50,000 vertebrate species (of which about 10,000 are birds and 4,000 are mammals, and about 26,000 are teleosts).

The IUCN states that:

> "Today, about 23% (1,130 species) of mammals and 12% (1,194 species) of birds are considered as threatened by IUCN.

Global biodiversity is being lost much faster than natural extinction due to changes in land use, unsustainable use of natural resources, invasive alien species, climate change and pollution among others.

Land conversion by humans, resulting in natural habitat loss, is most evident in tropical forests and is less intensive in temperate, boreal and arctic regions. Pollution from atmospheric nitrogen deposition is most severe in northern temperate areas close to urban centres; and the introduction of damaging alien species is usually brought about through patterns of human activity.

Species loss is also compounded by:

- the ongoing growth of human populations and unsustainable consumer lifestyles

- increasing production of waste and pollutants

- urban development

- international conflict."

Established in 1964, the IUCN's Red List of Threatened Species has evolved to become the world's most comprehensive information source on the global extinction risk status of animal, fungus and plant species.

The IUCN Red List is a critical indicator of the health of the world's biodiversity. Far more than a list of species and their status, it is a powerful tool to inform and catalyse action for biodiversity conservation and policy change, critical to protecting the natural resources we need to survive. It provides information about range, population size, habitat and ecology, use and/or trade, threats, and conservation actions that will help inform necessary conservation decisions.

The IUCN Red List is currently as follows (in descending order of priority):

- Extinct

- Extinct in the wild

- Regionally extinct

- Critically endangered

- Endangered

- Vulnerable

- Conservation dependent

- Near threatened

- Least concern

- Data deficient.

Of the twenty or so species of Danio on the IUCN Red List, it is encouraging to see that a number are of "Least doncern", although it might be argued that that status as achieved by *Danio rerio*, *Danio kerri* and *Danio choprai* might be down to the conservation efforts of freshwater aquarists.

Despite this success, it is salutary to note that a number of Danio species are endangered or vulnerable, and that quite a few are data deficient, arguably because they are so rare. In addition, the "Least concern" status is deceiving, because the numbers of all these Danios is nevertheless declining.

It is the responsibility of every aquarist to understand where the species of fish they are keeping sits on the Red List, and to act accordingly, also taking into account their responsibilities under the Animal Welfare Act 2006.

The 2021 population of my favourite Danio, *Danio rerio*, is described as follows on the Red List:

> "It is difficult to assess the population of the species. It is not common in the natural water bodies. It breeds easily in nature. Aquarists have also artificially bred the fish successfully. In Nepal the catch per unit effort (CPUE) of this species is up to 1.88%. In Arunachal Pradesh the catch rate is 1.9% (Tamang et al. 2007).
>
> **There is a continuing decline in area, extent and/or quality of habitat.**
>
> The species is an annual species. Adults inhabit streams, canals, ditches, ponds and beels occur in slow-moving to stagnant standing water bodies, particularly rice-fields and lower reaches of streams common in rivulets at foot hills. Feed on worms and small crustaceans, also on insect larvae. Breed all year round. Spawning is induced by temperature and commences at the onset of the monsoon season. Food availability also acts as cue for breeding."

What is an aquarium but a zoo, safari park, or wildlife reserve in microcosm? It is our duty to preserve these species and do our best for conservation. By creating biotope aquariums and supportive captive breeding programmes, aquarists are doing their bit to conserve – in much the same way as a zoo – the fish they love together with a facsimile of their environments and habitats.

There are those who might argue that this approach is invalid: that habitats should be developed exclusively in the wild and fish left to enjoy their wild state. The Born Free Foundation, founded by Will Travers, might argue this approach. But I would argue that, while such a position might be justified in a perfect world, this is not a perfect world and while species are creeping up the Red List and their habitats destroyed, a captive aquarium approach does its bit to preserve the genetics of declining species.

The late Dr Victoria Braithwaite discusses the issue thus[8]:

> "There is a growing trend for fish to be part of visual displays in public places such as shopping centers or restaurants; waiting rooms in doctors' surgeries or hospital outpatient areas increasingly incorporate displays of small tanks with various fish species. They are often considered to add a calming influence. Is it ethical to have fish on display in shopping malls or doctors' surgeries? Given the impressive moving images that can be displayed on television screens or computer monitors there are potential alternatives, but whether such substitutes have the same calming influence as the real thing has yet to be investigated. On a larger scale, public aquaria are regarded as valuable revenue-generating tourist attractions. The welfare of the fish we house and maintain in these facilities is beginning to be queried. In comparison to other areas where we interact with fish, there is almost nothing known about the effects of captivity and how the fish cope with brightly lit areas crowded, noisy, and bustling with activity.
>
> A number of studies have considered the welfare and ethics of zoo animals, and these arguments will relate to captive fish in public aquaria. The sourcing of fish for such displays is a welfare concern as the majority of fish on display are wild caught and are not reared in captivity. Thus issues of supply and transport arise in addition to how fish cope with being moved from the wild to captivity.
>
> In terrestrial zoo animals, like tigers, elephants and polar bears, boredom, frustration, and enclosures too small and too plain sometimes lead to 'stereotypies'—repetitive actions or movements performed over and over again. Likewise, sharks and other fish species that typically have large home ranges, or make long distance migrations, also show stereotypies in public aquaria. These behaviours are not necessarily painful but they do represent a welfare concern because they are expressions of frustration on the animal's part, and certain repetitive actions that involve contact with walls or other structures can lead to the fish rubbing and damaging their skin tissue. Finding ways to enrich and add variety to an environment appropriately, can help alleviate boredom in zoo enclosures. This has yet to be tried for fish in aquaria. Careful choice of which species to house in public aquaria, and avoiding species with known large home ranges would probably help to prevent the development of stereotypies.
>
> Whether it is ethical to house animals in zoos simply for our entertainment has been debated many times. Over recent years there has been a shift in the justification for zoos, with more recent arguments focusing on the role of

---

8   Braithwaite, Victoria. Do Fish Feel Pain? (pp. 172-174). OUP Oxford. Kindle Edition.

'God creating the birds and the fishes', by Martin de Vos (1532-1603)

zoos in conservation projects. Changes in the natural environment through climate change, overexploitation, and anthropogenic disturbance are taking their toll on many different fish populations. Public aquaria have barely been previously considered as conservation tools, but this may be a role to which they could contribute to in the future. We are becoming increasingly skilled in breeding various species of fish in captivity, a beneficial spin-off that aquaculture has provided, but the diversity of fish and their many different reproductive strategies mean there is still a lot to learn before we could consider aquaria to be significant contributors to some sort of biological ark."

What responsible hobby aquarists must do in this regard, then, as I have said before, is to attend to the welfare of their fish, and ensure they do not plunder the reserves of the planet but engage in captive breeding programmes with respect to the fish which they desire. Abusing fish by, for instance, indulging in fish-in cycling and stocking, packing and transporting from the wild should on the whole be fundamentally discouraged.

The importance of the conservation of freshwater fish is reinforced in an important report issued in March 2021 by WWF and a group of conservation NGOs (including Shoal) entitled *The World's Forgotten Fishes*. The report highlights the fact that one in three freshwater fish is threatened with extinction, and that by 2020 eighty freshwater species had been eradicated. The report emphasises the role aquarists can play in conservation by preserving endangered species and educating conservationists, as well as highlighting the need for aquarists to behave responsibly in their habits.

This is not the place to discuss the report in more detail, but those who are interested might Google "The World's Forgotten Fishes" to read it. *Practical Fishkeeping* also published an interesting article on the subject in its June 2021 edition, entitled "Overlooked and Underappreciated: The World's Forgotten Fishes."

So far so good. But what is the philosophical basis for conservation? At one level it is a purely selfish endeavour. Where would humankind be if all our natural habitats were destroyed and all the exotic species extinguished? What sort of a barren world would we live in? What concrete carpark globe would we be handing down to our grandchildren? Let alone considering how we might tackle the implications of climate change and the alleged increase of the propensity for pandemics in such a world.

The humanists might say that we have a pragmatic duty to preserve the planet for the benefit of humanity, and for the furtherance of the interests and utility-based rights of its fauna and flora. This is not such a far cry from the Christian approach to conservation. *Genesis*, Chapter 1[9] states:

> **Verses 20–23:** And God said, "Let the water teem with living creatures, and let birds fly above the earth across the vault of the sky. So God created the great creatures of the sea and every living thing with which the water teems and that moves about in it according to their kinds, and every winged bird according to its kind. And God saw that it was good. God blessed them and said "Be fruitful and increase in number and fill the water in the seas and let the birds increase on the earth. And there was evening and there was morning – the fifth day.
>
> **Verse 28 (of mankind):** God blessed them, and said to them, "Be fruitful and increase in number; fill the earth and subdue it. Rule over the fish in the sea and the birds in the sky and over every living creature that moves on the ground."

There are a number of things to note about these passages:

- God blesses fish and requires that they are fruitful and increase in number

- God requires mankind to rule over the fish of the sea. But what is "rule"? Rule comes with obligations as well as rights, as any just ruler will tell you. Looking, for instance, at a basic feudal overlordship, the Lord gives the people protection and enough land to prosper in return for their fealty and their obligation to fight for him

- The net result of all this is, in my view, the notion of "custodianship". Mankind is the custodian of nature, and has an obligation to promote the

---

9   *Holy Bible,* New International Version.

fulfilment of God's blessing on it – i.e. that it should be fruitful and increase in number.[10]

So, in sum, responsible aquarists should be proud of their aquariums and the part they play in conservation and the cosmic plan.

---

10 This is not the place for a discussion of Creationism, or the question of the extent to which the first creation story is a primitive metaphor for evolution couched in a way that people of the Second Millennium BCE could understand. I would just mention, however, that it is in my view astounding how accurate the account is in terms of its broad depiction of Big Bang theory and evolution as we currently perceive it. How could the peoples of the Second Millennium BCE possibly have understood the concepts of evolution or the Big Bang even if they had been immaculately explained?

7

The beautiful fish: a loving profile of the zebra danio

To my mind the zebra danio is to ichthyology what football is to sport: the beautiful game; the beautiful fish.

The zebra danio (*Danio rerio*), or zebrafish as it is often known, is the ~~stalking horse~~ stalwart of many cycling tanks suffering from "New Tank Syndrome[11]". Hardy, collegiate and gentle, it can seemingly put up with anything. In my case, when I was conducting fish-in cycling for my experimental 40-litre tank, my four "suicide squad" zebra danios put up with uncomfortably high ammonia and nitrite levels of 4ppm. It tolerates extremes of pH and gH and a wide spectrum of water temperatures. It can live up to four years and prefers the company of a shoal of at least six individuals.

For many, once the zebra danio's heavy lifting is done and the tank is cycled, the fish themselves are soon forgotten and superseded by seemingly more colourful species. For myself, I fell in love with the humble zebra danio, and chose to have a shoal of six of so as the centrepiece of my 40-litre tank. To me the zebra danio is a thing of beauty, rendered all the more wonderful by its compliant hard work in the quest for a balanced tank.

For those who doubt this, consider the zebra danio closely. It is not drab like its erstwhile cousin the blue danio (which has recently fallen somewhat out of favour for that reason). It has five horizontal dark blue-black lines along its flank, interspersed with shimmering silver. It has a characterful terminal mouth. It has a powerful caudal fin, with ray strands like lace, which it whips up to accelerate playful bursts of speed. It has a personality to beguile the most hard-hearted, and which in each case speaks out through the shoaling mayhem with ease. In

---

11 See Appendix 2 for a description of "New Tank Syndrome" (NTS).

summary, it is a miraculous beauty of nature, four centimetres of beguiling joy. It is, in my view, a much-overlooked treasure, a small shoal of which should find a home in every community tank.

The zebra danio's range in the wild stretches from Pakistan to Northern India, to Bangladesh, to Burma and to Nepal. It is often found in lentic habitats such as wetlands and paddy fields, as well as in some lotic environments such as flowing rivers and streams. The word *danio* itself means "of the paddy field" in Bangla.

Zebra Danio *(Danio rerio)*

It is an ovuliparous egglayer and is easy to breed, making it an excellent specimen for captive breeding, so there is no excuse for capturing it from the wild.

Nathan Hill, editor of *Practical Fishkeeping*, has written the following of the humble zebra danio[12]:

"We know more about laboratory *Danio rerio* than wild strains. We know captivity has altered their selective pressures, so that farmed Zebras will have a higher fecundity (ability to produce offspring) than wild fish, while the latter exhibit a far greater degree of predator avoidance and restlessness than captive ones.

Wild *D. rerio* inhabit slow moving water, typically in floodplains, oxbows, slow streams and established rice paddies, preferring an older paddy to a newer one. Any sluggish body with a heavily silted bottom, or sometimes gravel and cobbles, will become home.

---

12   *Zebra Danios. Used, Abused, Unique.*

International Space Station

Seasonally they make their way to temporary streams called *nalas*, the result of monsoon weather, to spawn. For a long time they were considered lowland inhabitants, but recent expeditions have found them at 1,800m/5,900ft. *D. rerio* are predated in the wild but fish don't seem to be the dominant consumers. Considering that they are close to snakeheads (*Channa sp.*), Needlefish (*Xenetodon*), Knifefish (*Notopterus*) and *Mystus bleekeri*, it seems odd that so many end up inside kingfishers and herons and not so much in other fish."

And it's not just in the wild and in tanks that the zebra danio excels. It is also a stalwart of the laboratories, a mainstay of biomedical research. As recently as 2019 it was stated in a research paper[13] that:

"Because of its fully sequenced genome, easy genetic manipulation, high fecundity, external fertilization and rapid development, and nearly transparent embryo, zebrafish are a unique model animal for biomedical research, including studies of biological processes and human diseases. Zebrafish have all the main organs involved in the process of metabolism and can be used to study several human metabolic disorders such as nonalcoholic fatty liver disease, type 2 diabetes mellitus, dyslipidemia, and other hepatic diseases. With innovation and improvement of molecular techniques, zebrafish will continue to be an important biomedical model in the future."

As part of this family of experiments, the zebra danio has even found its way into space, when Japanese astronauts took it to the International Space Station in January 2015. NASA's Johnson Space Center[14] published an online article about this, and the circumstances are so interesting, and the zebra danio's moment of glory in the firmament so deserving of celebration, it is worth quoting the article in part:

"Although zebrafish are not deadlifting weights in orbit, they are helping researchers learn about muscle changes during their stay aboard the International Space Station. This impacts not only the fish, but also the crew and can have implications for Earth-related muscle challenges too. The Japan Aerospace Exploration Agency's JAXA Zebrafish Muscle Investigation

---

13 'The use of zebrafish (*Danio rerio*) as biomedical models,' Tsegay Teame et al, June 2019.
14 Laura Niles, *Zebrafish Flex their Muscles for Research Aboard the International Space Station.* International Space Station Program Science Office and Public Affairs Office, NASA's Johnson Space Center.

observes the effects of microgravity on the zebrafish, *Danio rerio*, a tropical freshwater fish belonging to the minnow family.

This research has the potential to lead to new drugs or treatments for patients on extended bed rest or with limited mobility. In addition to the potential human benefits, results from this study could aid researchers in developing countermeasures for muscle weakness in astronauts living in microgravity during extended missions...

Zebra danios shoaling

...Researchers study zebrafish because of their transparency compared to other fish. Scientists use transgenic zebrafish, which express fluorescence proteins inside the body to obtain three dimensional imaging of skeletal muscle and tendon tissues within the zebrafish. This means that the zebrafish contain DNA that is inserted experimentally...

...A total of 18 zebrafish were launched to the space station. Five fish returned alive on a previous Soyuz spacecraft and some chemically preserved fish will be returned with the completion of the fifth SpaceX commercial resupply mission. The Zebrafish Muscle research team will compare gene expression – the process of determining a cell's function – profiles between fish flown in space and control fish on Earth. Specifically, they will look to see if fish muscle deteriorates in space and recovers upon return to the ground. The team also will examine if fish tendon is sensitive to microgravity."

Despite the zebra danio's scientific remit, there is still room for artistic inspiration around it. You might have thought that the poetry in the previous chapter was the last word in poems about freshwater fish. But you would be wrong, for the humble zebrafish has even inspired poetry all of its own. I've often hit the pillow wondering what my zebra danios would be doing while they slept. Well, perhaps the answer lies in the poem below.

Do yourself a favour: once your tank is cycled, don't overlook the zebra danio. Buy a shoal and you'll never look back.

A **Wish** about a **Zebrafish**

by Gershon Wolf

*Here's a question that I wish
to ask about a zebrafish
No, not about how it looks ~
I can use the Internet or books*

*I want to know just how despite
missing eyelids to block its sight
this little fish of black and white
manages to sleep at night*

*So I looked and found some information
regarding homeostatic regulation
And if you ask me what that is
I'll reply with this analysis*

*We see in most land-based creatures
this constantly occurring feature
That if deprived of sleep one night
animals tend to set it right*

*They make up their sleep the next few rounds
a trait the scientists call 'sleep rebound'
And now I have some news for you ~
That's precisely what zebrafish do*

*As well, when asleep they float in place
as if they're staring off into space
They float horizontal or head up slightly
and I learned, they do this nightly*

*So, I'm happy that my wish was granted
~ and that zebrafish don't sleep slanted*

8

Planning for a bigger tank

At the time of writing, I had not yet purchased my bigger tank. To that extent some aspects of this book could be perceived as a work of fiction. But I planned and researched my 240-litre tank meticulously, so this chapter and those aspects should be approached as an idyllic depiction of how setting up and establishing the tank would go in a perfect world. When I do establish my bigger tank (hopefully very soon after publication), any aberrations or deviations from what is described will be set out in the Second Edition.

I learned from setting up and establishing my 40-litre experimental tank that planning is everything. If I hadn't learned that lesson through experience, I learned it through theory: both *The Perfect Aquarium* by Jeremy Gay and *Aquascaping* by George Farmer emphasise that planning is key to success in setting up an aquarium.

My first task was to determine the size of my new tank. I was initially drawn to a Fluval Shaker 252, but I eventually decided that it was a bit too broad for my requirements, and I opted instead for the slightly sleeker Fluval New Roma 240. It seemed to me that this tank was large enough to give me a serious challenge, but not so large as to be an overstatement. The Fluval New Roma 240 gives you a "turnkey" solution, and comes with a hood, LED lighting, a heater and a Fluval 307 external canister filter that is connected to the tank via an intake and outtake tube drilled through the glass at the bottom.

On the whole it's an excellent tank, but it has two problems, both to do with filtration. First, a number of people suggest that the 307 filter does not give sufficient flow, and that it should be swopped out for a 407. And secondly, and this may be part of the first problem, the intake and outtake tubes are located beside each other in the rear right hand corner, which again is not conducive to good flow. For myself, I chose to swop out the 307 for the 407. Having chosen my tank, I then sat down with a cup of coffee and, with my experimental 40-litre tank before me as inspiration, I listed out all the other equipment I would need to commence fishless cycling with my 240-litre tank, and also sketched out my stocking requirements once my 240-litre tank had cycled.

The plan I devised is set out at Appendix 1. Once I was happy with it, I took the Underground train to Maidenhead Aquatics and talked my plan through with the very helpful manager there. He guided me on a number of issues. Primarily he gave me good advice on water chillers. In Belfast when I had my community tank the summers were typically much cooler than they are in London, and it concerned me that often in the South East of England the temperatures can these days reach nearly 40°C for a couple of weeks a year, especially in August.

Figure 3: Fluval New Roma 240-litre tank

Fluval New Roma 240-litre tank	Matching walnut finish cabinet
14.5 Watt LED lighting unit	Hood
Heater	Fluval 307 external canister filter
Swop out Fluval 307 for Fluval 407 external canister filter	Intake and outtake apparatus

Fishkeepers are usually concerned with heating the water to tropical temperatures – 24 to 28°C, say – but what if the ambient temperature hits 40°C? What happens to your water temperature then, and what of fish that prefer cooler tropical temperatures like zebra danios? Perhaps a water chiller was the answer.

I looked online at a prominent retail store and to my horror water chillers came in at hundreds of pounds and would have been the second most expensive item on my list other than my turnkey tank itself. The manager at Maidenhead Aquatics reassured me that everything would be alright even with higher temperatures for a few days. I didn't need a water chiller, but what I could do was float a bag of ice cubes or freeze some water in a PET bottle and put them in the tank if things got really bad. I sought a second opinion from the *UK Aquatic Plant Society* Forum, and the manager's approach was confirmed. Equally, someone on the Forum suggested that it was unlikely that tap water would exceed 26°C even in very hot weather, so frequent water changes might also do the trick.

The next thing I had to decide was how "high-tech" or "low-tech" my tank was going to be. As far as I can see, this question is a function of three elements:

- Whether or not I was going to inject CO_2 into my tank
- How bright/intense the lighting in my tank should be
- How heavily planted my tank should be.

I had already decided that heavy planting was going to be a feature of my biotope, and that, while my fish stock was its most fundamental aspect, planting was also important. I am heavily influenced by Diana Walstad's book *The Ecology of the Planted Aquarium*, and have come to the view that CO_2 injection might not be necessary in a well-balanced tank even if it is heavily planted. On top of this, I was also aware that CO_2 injection can be an expensive occupation (not to say bulky!) and precarious for the lives of fish if the CO_2 levels are not managed properly.

Someone told me that a compromise was to squirt some carbon enhancer into the tank, but George Farmer warned me off this in *Aquascaping*, explaining that such remedies can be poisonous, and this was also confirmed on the *UK Aquatic Plant Society* Forum. (See, too, Chapter 12 in this regard).

I therefore decided not to pursue an enhanced CO_2 or carbon approach, but to try instead for a well-balanced aquarium. The one thing I would do, however, was ensure that my lighting was as bright and intense as possible and that it was turned on for eight hours a day. For these purposes it is arguable that the 14.5 watt lighting solution provided with my New Roma 240 may not be sufficient, and I am considering swapping it out for a higher-wattage Aquasky solution.

Having made these decisions, and having also decided to conduct fishless cycling for all the reasons discussed elsewhere, only the fun bit remained: deciding upon planting and fish stock.

With regard to planting, I drew up a shortlist of plants that I might include in my tank (see also Appendix 1):

Foreground/Carpeting
- *Hellanthium tenellum* "Green"
- *Micranthemum* "Monte Carlo"
- *Hemianthus callitrichoides* "Cuba"

Midground
- *Cryptocoryne wendtii* "Green"
- *Cryptocoryne* X *willistii*
- *Pogostemon erectus*

Background
- Green cabomba (*Cabomba caroliniana*)
- Amazon sword (*Echinodorus* "blehrae")
- *Bacopa caroliniana*
- *Hygrophilia* "siamensis 53B"
- *Limnophilia hippuroides*

Moss: one type of moss to glue to the rocks, e.g. Taxyphillum "Spiky"
Epiphyte: I had no experience of Epiphyte plants, so I would seek advice from the manager of Maidenhead Aquatics, Morden, about one or two easy species to select.

Bronze corydoras *(Corydoras aenous)*

Most of the above specimens are recommended in *Aquascaping* or *The Perfect Aquarium*. When buying these plants I had decided that I would take the easy option and buy whatever of them were available at Maidenhead Aquatics at the relevant time. I conducted a recce and determined that about half of the species of relevant plants were available when I visited.

It then only remained to plan out my fish stocking. As is well known, the crude rule of thumb is 1 cm of fish for each litre of water. The level is higher (1.5 cm fish per litre) for an aquarium with external canister filter filtration, but I am not a fan of cramming an aquarium to the gunnels, and I chose to stick to the 1 cm rule. That would allow me 240 cm of fish.

Well, it can be no surprise by now that I wanted a large shoal of zebra danios. But I wanted to contrast them against two other Danio species shoals (see next chapter) and a moderate shoal of pepper corydoras. I also wanted to stock the tank with Amano shrimp and red cherry shrimp, which, due to their proclivities, score 0 when calculating stocking, and the rule of thumb here is that you can allow one shrimp for every five litres of water.

I had a long-list of species, but eventually opted for the selection shown in Figure 4. This would give me a total of 165 points, meaning that my tank would be stocked at just over 65% capacity. This was perfect for my requirements. Proportionately, my fish stock could be represented in Figure 5.

Having made this determination, I rang my good friend Mick, who was a builder. I agreed with him a day for him to help me collect the tank and equipment from Maidenhead Aquatics in his van, and to help me erect the cabinet. Since it was destined to carry the weight of over 240 kg of water, substrate and rocks, it had to be put up properly.

Figure 4: Species selection for new 240-litre tank

Species	Quantity	Adult length
Zebra danio	12	5 cm
Glowlight danio	10	2.5 cm
Gold ring danio	10	3 cm
Pepper corys	4	5.5 cm
Bronze corys	4	7 cm
Amano shrimp	10	3 cm – 6 cm
Red cherry shrimp	10	4 cm

Figure 5: Proportionate analysis of fish stock for new 240-litre tank

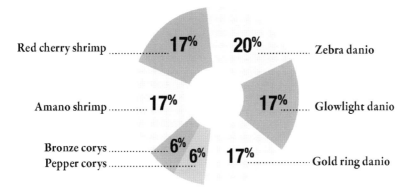

Mick came round to discuss logistics over a coffee, and, while he was there, he inspected the floor to ensure that it was sufficiently load-bearing, and the electrics close to where the tank would be sited to ensure everything was safe: electrics and water don't mix! I devised an action plan with Mick:

- Purchase equipment, tank and plants
- Transport home
- Erect cabinet
- Place tank on cabinet
- Instal external filter
- Add substrate (doesn't need rinsing because it is Tropica Aquarium Soil)

Blue danio *(Danio kerri)*

- Install heater
- Aquascaping:
    - Install rocks
    - Install bogwood
    - Glue on moss and plant Epiphyte plants
- Fill tank 30%
- Plant up plants
- Add substrate fertiliser capsules
- Fill up remaining 70% of tank
- Add Tap Safe
- Switch on heater and external filter
- Leave tank overnight
- Add in Dr Tim's One and Only
- Add in Dr Tim's First Defense
- Add in liquid fertiliser
- Have a well-earned beer.

After leaving this for a couple of hours, I could grab my ammonia bottle and add the requisite number of drops of ammonia to commence fishless cycling.

My planning was complete: time to prepare.

9

Preparing for a Danio Dreamworld[15]

In an earlier chapter, I set out the challenges I encountered in setting up my new 40-litre experimental tank. Although I had been a keen aquarist for many years as a teenager, thirty five years later the techniques of the hobby had moved on and I embarked on a steep learning curve.

Emerging from the tribulations of "New Tank Syndrome" and the trials of fish-in cycling, I eventually felt ready to do what I had always intended – indulge myself in a new 240-litre tank. Even before I presented my credit card and purchased this monster, my experience with my 40-litre experimental tank taught me that planning is everything. So, as I explained in the previous chapter, the first thing I did was sit down with a pencil and paper and plot out a biotope for the tank.

I had initially thought I would establish an Amazonian tank with schools of neon tetras (*Paracheirodon innesi*), cardinal tetras (*Paracheirodon axelrodi*) and some sort of *Corydoras*. But when fish-in cycling with my experimental tank, I fell in love again with the humble zebra danio (*Danio rerio*), and I decided instead that I would establish a Danio-friendly biotope and stock the tank exclusively with various species of Danios, especially since there have been a number of recent discoveries (e.g. *Danio tinwini*). Species I shortlisted for the tank included zebra danios (*Danio rerio*), glowlight danios (*Danio choprai*), pearl danios (*Danio albolineatus*), panther danios (*Danio aesculapii*), blue danios (*Danio kerri*) and gold ring danios (*Danio tinwini*).

Wikipedia discusses the taxonomy of Danios as follows:

> "The name "danio" comes from the Bangla name *dhani*, meaning "of the rice field". *Danio* was described in the early 19th century by Francis Hamilton.

---

15   This chapter is based upon an article I wrote that at the time of writing had yet to be scheduled for publication. There is a little duplication with some of the material in other chapters, for which I make no apology.

Two of the species included by him in the genus still remain valid—*D. dangila* and *D. rerio*. About a century later (1916) and with many more species described in the meantime, the genus was split; the larger species into *Danio* and the smaller species into the genus *Brachydanio*. In 1991, though, the two genera were recombined; most larger species formerly within the genus *Danio* have now been reclassified into the genus *Devario*. Also, *Brachydanio* is now a junior synonym of *Danio*."

Gold ring danio *(Danio tinwini)*

Typically, my intended Danios would all be no more than five centimetres in length, most no more than three centimetres. Males are usually torpedo-shaped while females are slightly larger and more full-bellied. Danios are shoaling fish and ideally should not be kept in schools of fewer than six specimens. They typically have terminal mouths, perfect for feeding at every level.

Danios' ranges are typically based in Asia and a depiction of the extent of the various ranges and habitats of my intended Danios is set out at Figure 6. Figure 7 sets out a map indicating the general geographical range of the genus *Danio*.

The exceptions to the coherence of my intended Danio biotope would be that I would stock the substrate with a school of bronze corys (*Corydoras aeneus*) and pepper corys (*Corydoras paleatus*), and the planting would be more eclectic and reflect a more global view than the Danios' home turf.

As far as vegetation was concerned, the tank would be heavily planted and would be traditional with no regional observance. Background planting would be dominated by cabomba (*Cabomba caroliniana*), vallisneria (*Vallisneria americana*) and *Micranthemum orbiculatum*, while mid-ground plants would include Amazon sword plants (*Echinodorus bleheri*) and crypts (*Cryptocoryne wendtii*), amongst others. Planting of fast-growing background plants would concentrate around the sides of the tank to give the Danios room to school and pick up bursts of speed.

Figure 6: Range and habitat of selected Danio species

Name	Range	Habitat
Danio rerio	Bhutan, India, Nepal, Pakistan	Moderately flowing streams and stagnant pools such as rice paddies
Danio kerri	Malaysia	Island streams and pools
Danio tinwini	Myanmar	Only found in Mogaung Chaung (Mogaung stream), Myitkyina District, Myanmar which is a tributary of the Irrawaddy
Danio albolineatus	Sumatra, Myanmar, Thailand	Found along the surface of small, clear rivers and hill streams
Danio choprae	Myanmar	Moderately flowing streams and stagnant pools
Danio aesculapii	Myanmar	Endemic

Figure 7: Map showing the general distribution of the genus Danio

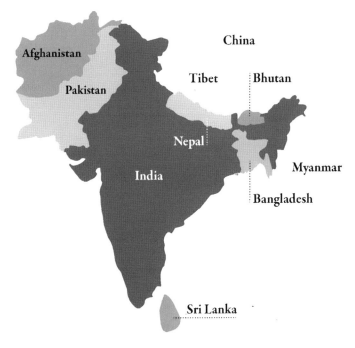

Figure 8: Non-exclusive equipment[16] list for new 240-litre tank

Tank and matching cabinet	Appropriate substrate and rocks
External filter and carbon media change x2	Heater
Swap out Fluval 407 external canister filter	Spare heater
Airstone and pump	Wavemaker
Hood	Lighting rig
2D Background	Bottled ammonia and fish flakes for ammonia production
Live bacteria solution	Dechlorinator and fish destressing solution
Sundries such as filter sock, test kits, nets, plant fertiliser, syphons, vacuums, etc	Live plants

The choice of substrate gave me pause for thought. In my experimental tank I had used a proprietary aquarium soil, which while excellent for plant growth tended to soften the water and lower its pH, although only for a few months (according to the manufacturer). Because this was to be a Danio tank but was to have corys, I was aiming for a pH of 6.8–7.0 and for a cory-friendly substrate. Nevertheless, on the advice of my favourite fish store, I selected the same medium-grade aquarium soil that would also assist plant growth with the addition of both substrate and in-water fertilizer. Although this soil would buffer and soften the water for a time, it was unlikely to do so for more than three months.

I chose the most powerful filter I reasonably could. It cycles the tank at least five times an hour and provides a generous flow through the tank – very important since Danios' habitat in the wild is rivers. Given the size of the tank, I also budgeted for a wavemaker to place on the opposite side of the tank to the filter outlet to aid water flow and aeration.

I planned to buy a robust heater, with the aim of keeping the water temperature at 24°C. A non-exclusive list of key equipment I bought around my 240-litre tank is set out at Figure 8.

I planned to install an RO filter in our kitchen tap. The gH of water in London (where I live) is very hard. I knew that occasionally I would have to conduct water changes with RO water, but I was determined not to overdo it. One lesson I learned with my experimental tank was that if you use RO water all the time

---

16   Always be sure to read equipment instructions carefully, and to take particular care when handling electrical equipment. Remember that water and electricity present a particular hazard.

without mineral supplements your pH and gH plummet, and at one point my pH lowered to 6.0 which, apart from not being great for the Danios, is bad for growth of *Nitrosomonas* and *Nitrobacter* bacteria. Equally, too low a gH can adversely affect osmosis and leach salts from fish. Accordingly, I would use a balance of hard water and RO water to achieve a happy result.

The biggest lesson I learned with my experimental tank was (although not everyone would agree) to avoid fish-in cycling at all costs. It's extremely stressful on the fish and their owners if they love them. Accordingly, I determined to carry out fishless cycling utilizing a prominent proprietary live bacteria formula which would almost certainly cut several weeks off the cycling process.

Fishless cycling is a mystery to some, but in principle it is quite easy. The main ingredient is patience. Fishless cycling can take up to twelve weeks they say, but there are a number of measures you can take to make it much quicker.

First, you can introduce filter media and substrate from an established tank. This option was not open to me because I had to keep my experimental tank going until my 240-litre tank had cycled and I could transfer my zebra danios and I didn't know anyone who was breaking down an old tank. Secondly, you can use a live bacteria formula of which there are several on the market. These claim to reduce cycling time substantially, even dramatically. I used one in my 40-litre tank cycling and it did seem to cut the cycling time in half at least. For these purposes it's important to keep the pH and gH levels at the higher end and increase the temperature and ensure there are adequate minerals in the water to give the bacteria an enhanced opportunity to grow.

Glowlight danio *(Danio choprai)*

From my research it became clear that in my fishless cycling I could expect an ammonia (NH_3) spike, and then some days later a nitrite (NO_2) spike. This is mainly because the *Nitrosomonas* bacteria, which convert ammonia to nitrite, reproduce slightly faster than the *Nitrobacter* bacteria, which convert nitrite to nitrate (NO_3).

There is a debate about whether *Nitrosomonas* and *Nitrobacter* are in fact the correctly identified bacteria for aquariums in this regard, with the argument being that they are instead prevalent in water sewage plants where ammonia and nitrite levels are much higher. (Not being a microbiologist, I am not qualified to comment further on that debate, except to say that for the purposes of this book I will assume that *Nitrosomonas* and *Nitrobacter* are the correct bacteria because that still appears to be the most commonly held view.)

I now describe an example fishless cycling event. I would put the required drops of bottled ammonia and a few fish flakes into my new tank every other day and test the water for ammonia, nitrite and nitrate on alternate days. Measurements would proceed broadly to plan. Ammonia levels would spike in weeks two and three, while nitrite levels would spike in weeks three and four. Nitrate levels would very briefly peak at 40ppm, but quickly settle at 10-20ppm, a testament to the efficacy of a heavily planted tank. (This is well documented in Diana Walstad's heavily researched book, *The Ecology of the Planted Aquarium*.)

After five weeks – and still putting in my ammonia drops and fish flakes every other day – my ammonia level would reduce to <0.25ppm and my nitrite level had similarly reduced to about 0.25ppm. Now that's not perfect, because in each case the level should be 0ppm. But it would be a significant result. To be on the safe side I would wait a further week to be rewarded with both the ammonia and nitrite levels reducing to ≈ 0ppm.

An example depiction of the fluctuation in the ammonia, nitrite and nitrate levels of my 240-litre tank during the fishless cycling process is set out at Figure 9.

Out of an abundance of caution I would wait a further few days to ensure my tank was stable. And now it was time to stop artificially introducing ammonia and introduce my zebra danios from my experimental tank! I would catch them with a net and put them into a plastic bag with some water from my experimental tank as if I were buying fish from a store. I would float the bag on top of the water in my 240-litre tank to equalise the temperature, and then gradually mix the water every ten minutes for half an hour. And I would let them go.

I would check the ammonia and nitrite level daily for a few days, and once I was satisfied that there would be no substantial ammonia spike and the fish were thriving, I would go to the store and buy four more. Again I would test, and once I was happy with the new ammonia and nitrite levels I would keep introducing four fish at a time every few days from the store until my tank was stocked to my satisfaction. At the point I would commence weekly 25% water changes and monthly filter maintenance as normal, remembering to wash my filter media in a bucket of old tank water to ensure I did not kill the filter bacteria.

Figure 9: Example ammonia (NH_3), nitrite (NO_2) and nitrate (NO_3) fluctuations during a fishless cycle (with bacteria growth encouraged by the addition of live bacteria) using an API liquid test kit

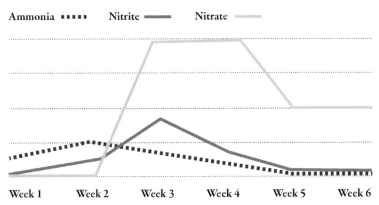

There are those who might say that this is all a bit of a palaver, and that there is nothing wrong with fish-in cycling. I sympathise that people want to get their fish tanks up and running as quickly as possible, and that five or so weeks is a long time to wait to be able to enjoy one's fish. Nevertheless, fish-in cycling requires the introduction of "suicide squads", some of which will almost inevitably die. Speaking for myself, when I conducted fish-in cycling I awoke each morning with a feeling of dread, expecting legions of dead fish to have succumbed: it was very stressful. I would much rather exercise patience and wait. My eventual reward will be a healthy, cycled Danio tank with a population of varying species of Danios – and no "New Tank Syndrome" to worry about!

Who can ask for more than that? As was said in the film *Finding Nemo*: "Fish are friends, not food!" We should exercise patience and caution and give them the easiest ride we can.

Finally, I should mention that I am sure there will be some who might feel that keeping Danios is not the most difficult challenge for a fishkeeper, especially when compared, say, to keeping discus fish or cichlids (or even, especially, marine fish for that matter). Danios are famously hardy and tolerant and forgiving of mistakes. But I keep fish for their beauty, character and personality rather than their difficulty. As I have reiterated almost ad infinitum in this book, Danios are beautiful in their shimmering glory, characterful in bucketloads and resplendent in personality. The fact they are hardy is a happy coincidence.

10

Aquascaping and biotope integrity

Imagine you have just observed the most beautiful fish tank you have ever seen. You come away in wonder. But what do you remember? Do you remember the fish? That gorgeous red-tailed black shark? That oblong awkward discus? Or do you remember the Aquascape? That vivid green carpet of foreground planting? Or that amazing hardscape of lava rock jutting heavenwards with an intriguing piece of bogwood poking out behind it?

The bottom line is, nine times out of ten you can have all the fish you want, but unless they are complimented by an appropriate Aquascape, they will not be shown off to full advantage. To that extent, then, if you want an aquarium that looks complete, you can't have fish without Aquascaping and vice versa. Take that carpet of foreground planting, for instance. How beautiful is that when shown off against the shimmering red-blue of a tight shoal of neon tetras?

Someone once said that: "The greatest Fine Art of the future will be the making of a comfortable living from a small piece of land." This quote was actually, I think, about allotment gardening, but it could equally apply to Aquascaping. But the fulfilment of Aquascaping is more than the sum of its parts. For an Aquascape cannot be fulfilled without a complimentary biotope and fish. The perfect aquarium is a compromise between all three.

For instance, if a keen aquarist devises a complex high-tech Aquascape with difficult plants, he or she immediately faces compromises as far as fish are concerned:

- The fish may eat some of the plants

- The aquarist may choose to inject CO_2 into the tank to feed the plants, thus risking the fishes' health if injection is not managed properly

- Daily pruning of the plants may be necessary, thus disrupting the fish

- Higher-wattage lighting may be necessary to encourage the plants to grow

- Daily doses of waterborne fertilizer may be necessary

- Monthly doses of in-substrate fertilizer capsules may be necessary

- Phosphate levels become a concern, which may ultimately affect the fish and promote algae

- There are apocryphal stories of Aquascapers introducing shoals of fish into their Aquascapes just before photography. Because the fish are stressed, they shoal together more tightly thus producing a more impressive display, especially against a vivid green carpet of foreground planting.

For many, a compromise is appropriate. There is much debate about the contrast between so-called "high-tech" and "low-tech" systems. But what is wrong with a "mix and match" system? Just because you don't have CO_2 injection doesn't mean you can't have higher-wattage lighting combined with daily waterborne fertilizer doses and substrate fertilizer capsules. Just because you don't want an Aquascape that will win an international award, doesn't mean to say you can't have a meaningful Aquascape that is a pearl of great beauty.

A brilliant Aquascape

When I planned my Fluval New Roma 240-litre tank I planned an Aquascape of just such compromise. I chose hardy but beautiful red and green plants that were easy growers. I decided against CO_2 injection, but I selected a higher-wattage lighting rig and decided I would dose with in-water fertilizer every day as recommended by George Farmer in *Aquascaping*.

In the other direction, I compromised on my biotope. I had originally thought I would have a rockier biotope to reflect an Asian theme and select only Asian plants. But I soon came to believe that this would be quite boring and that I would want some bogwood in my tank, indicating a more Amazonian theme. The fish stocking was to comprise Danios and Corydoras, so there was a tension between those two environments.

The compromise was to have rocks and bogwood and not to be didactic with my choice of planting. I would have plants from throughout the world – it didn't matter where, as long as they looked beautiful and created a nice contrast. There would be a carpet of green foreground planting, as with many good Aquascapes, lots of midground crypts and Epiphyte plants and mosses, and a solid curtain of alternating red and green background plants.

I selected my rocks carefully, and I chose them both for their esoteric form and for their safety for the fish. So I chose light grey rock (because I wanted a light and airy feel to my tank that was not at all as foreboding as black or more laval rock might be) without seams of calcium or other chemical compounds. I chose my bogwood presoaked so I did not need to worry about it floating; and, again, I chose an esoteric shape that would sit nicely behind the rocks and in front of the background plant curtain. When eventually I came to set up my 240-litre tank, I would from this point get out my Superglue and glue the moss to the bogwood and jam the Epiphyte plants into the crevices between the rocks.

And, finally, I would pour in 33% of my water and begin to plant. There is no point in me describing how I would Aquascape my tank in detail. The whole subject has been brilliantly and exhaustively dealt with by George Farmer in his excellent book, *Aquascaping*. For those, however, who want to see the preliminary plans for my Aquascape and its planting, please see Appendix 1.

Once I had planted up, the Aquascape would probably look quite barren even though it had been heavily planted. It would take a month before the tank was more mature and I could have a proper impression of the fruits of my labours. Coincidentally, this timescale would more or less coincide with the completion of my fishless cycling, so my tank would then be ready to receive fish not only from the perspective of a mature filter, but also from that of a maturing Aquascape.

It would be a thing of beauty. But a mongrel. Like the best mongrels, it would have a soft heart. It would never win any prizes in an International Competition, but it would win a place in my soul. As William James once said: "We are like islands in the sea, separate on the surface but connected in the deep." The same is true for Aquascapes: a well-forged Aquascape is like a little submerged island with a causeway straight to the soul.

11

Cats, lateral lines, bagpipes and hoovers

It was Oliver Gaspirt who commented that "a fish tank is just interactive television for cats".

That begs a question. If you have cats, how amenable are they likely to be to your fish? I have two beautiful cats, and when I brought home my experimental 40-litre tank I was petrified for the first few days that I would come home and find one of them sitting seemingly innocently alongside it dabbling its paw in the water with a freshly chewed caudal fin poking out of its mouth.

Surprisingly, then, my cats showed absolutely no interest in my experimental tank. There were, I think, three main reasons for this. First, I placed the tank on a very high stand so it would have been extremely difficult – even for cats – to have leapt on top of it; secondly, the tank was quite small, so the surface area of the lid wasn't really conducive to a cat nap; and thirdly my tank was populated by small fish – Danios mostly – so perhaps they were too small to be attractive. If there had been a kissing gourami (*Helostoma temminckii*) in there it might have been different.

Things would change, however, when I brought home my 240-litre Fluval New Roma 240. The big problem here was that the relatively low cabinet height means that the tank's top would have just a nice surface area for a snooze and just at a nice jumping height. During fishless cycling – even with no fish in the tank – my cats would sit a yard away

Cat with fish in its eyes

from the tank, mischievously swishing their tails, jaws salivating, as they eye it up. I will be reminded of John Keats' poem "To Mrs Reynolds' Cat":

To Mrs Reynolds' Cat
by John Keats (1795–1821)

Cat! *who hast pass'd thy grand climacteric,*
How many mice and rats hast in thy days
Destroy'd? How many tit bits stolen? Gaze
With those bright languid segments green, and prick
Those velvet ears – but pr'ythee do not stick
Thy latent talons in me – and upraise
Thy gentle mew – and tell me all thy frays,
Of fish and mice, and rats and tender chick.
Nay, look not down, nor lick thy dainty wrists –
For all thy wheezy asthma – and for all
Thy tail's tip is nick'd off – and though the fists
Of many a maid have given thee many a maul,
Still is that fur as soft, as when the lists
In youth thou enter'dest on glass bottled wall.

One might as well ask the question "How many guppies and mollies hast in thy days destroyed?"

So, what was I going to do about this? Well, as yet the cats have behaved and no Danios have been swallowed, but I have a plan if the day ever comes. Do you know those plastic spikes they use on railway stations to stop pigeons roosting in the crevices? Well, I'm going to buy some of those and stick them to the roof of my tank, and that should do it. If that doesn't work I might buy some corrugated iron and construct a feline "peace wall" to separate out the potential combatants. Other than that, I'll just have to stuff my cats with Felix Ocean Feasts in Jelly in the hopes they are so sated they couldn't be bothered with my shrimp and Corydoras.

The next problem I had with my experimental tank revolved around lateral lines, the swimbladder and the Weberian Apparatus. Britannica.com describes the lateral line system in fish as follows:

> "The lateral line system allows the fish to determine the direction and rate of water movement. The fish can then gain a sense of its own movement, that of nearby predators or prey, and even the water displacement of stationary objects."

Salute to the Zebra Danios

March

Robert Porter

'Salute to the Zebra Danios', by Robert Porter

This makes fish extremely sensitive to vibrations. On top of this, many fish have a structure called the Weberian Apparatus. *The Aquarium Masterclass* describes the Weberian Apparatus as:

> "... a structure of fine bones that connects the swimbladder to the inner ear. Because the swimbladder acts as a drum and amplifier, this allows the fish to detect sounds that the inner ear alone would be unable to hear."

So, as well as being extremely sensitive to vibrations, fish are also sensitive to noise.

What a pity, then, that the room in which my experimental tank sits has a deep pile carpet that needs hoovering twice a week. And what an even greater pity that, keen bagpiper that I am, I typically play my bagpipes in that room.

While my fish were suffering during fish-in cycling, I forbad anyone from hoovering around the fish. Sadly, though, the dust and debris piled up, and one day my wife grabbed the hoover and surreptitiously sallied forth. I raced up to the tank to observe the fishes' reaction, but to my surprise and relief they seemed totally oblivious to the whole operation.

Sadly, the same could not be said of my bagpipes. There is an instrument in bagpiping called the "practice chanter" that looks and sounds a bit like the Indian instrument, the Shenai. It is designed to allow pipers to practise their music without skirling up the pipes and disturbing the whole neighbourhood, and it has about one tenth of the sound volume of the pipes themselves.

Well, when I played a *Piobaireachd* (lament) on my practice chanter my Danios went berserk. I stopped at once and sadly accepted I would have to find somewhere else to practise, or else muffle my practice chanter down so much that it sounded like a Kazoo. When I related this to my pipe tutor, an extremely successful piper called Dr Peter McCalister who had won the gold medal at Inverness in 2019, he was most amused. He approved of my composition of a 4/4 march in honour of my fishes' discomfort called *Salute to the Zebra Danios* (see above).

Cats, hoovers, bagpipes and all, it would seem as though my fish are in for a precarious time. But they survive to this day.

12

Top Tips

Keep an aquarist's diary

There are a number of things which proved invaluable to me when taking up fishkeeping again after so long. These included assiduously reading the core textbooks and taking advice from experienced aquarists. But one of the things that was crucial in this regard was the little black notebook I bought from Sainsbury's.

As soon as I ran it through the till I promised myself I would keep a daily account of all my encounters with my experimental 40-litre tank at least until it had cycled. It was a bold commitment, because that kind of promise is more often honoured in the breach. But to my surprise I kept my pledge.

Every morning I would test the pH and gH (and sometimes kH) and the ammonia, nitrite and nitrate levels and write them up in my notebook. I would record every water change, every dose of fertiliser, live bacteria, StressCoat, First Defense, Tapsafe and Seachem Neutral Regulator. Every feed was recorded, together with my assessment of whether I had overfed or underfed. I would take a daily temperature reading and note from a visual inspection that the filter was working. Every time I cleaned the filter and its impeller I would make a note. Every pruning of my *Cabomba* was recorded. Every time I made a mistake (or even did something right, or had a triumph), I would jot it down.

This might sound obsessive, but it was in fact only temporary, to ensure that I was learning while my tank was cycling. I remember the day my tank cycled and my ammonia reading came up yellow and my nitrite a translucent light blue. I had fulfilled my vow and would not record my data so assiduously again until I was fishless cycling my new 240-litre tank. I still tested the water every day for a week or so to ensure the tank had settled and to monitor for any ammonia and nitrite spikes when I added new fish stock, but after that I lightened up a lot and began to test the water only every other day.

The net result of all this diarising is that I learnt lessons well and they stuck. Also, I could spot trends in my fishkeeping, and in particular had a record of the behaviour of my water quality during fish-in cycling. Again, I could see how I was improving as an aquarist over time. Finally, my aquarist's diary performed the function of a sort of *aide memoire* when it came to write this book.

Keep an aquarist's diary. It costs you only five minutes a day and the price of a basic notebook. And it is invaluable.

Red cherry shrimp *(Neocaridina davidi)*

Don't kill your fish with kindness by using RO water

In London where I live the water is very hard. When I had lived in Belfast as a teenager, the last time I had kept tropical freshwater fish, the water was soft, so hardness was not an issue.

Give the London problem I resolved at an early stage to fill my tank with RO water. So, it only being a 40-litre tank and not having an RO filter attached to the kitchen tap, I purchased a water filter jug and diligently filled buckets of water from it whenever I filled my tank or conducted a water change.

I thought I was doing the best thing by my fish. But in fact I was killing them. The problem was twofold. First. from the perspective of pH, the combination of Tropica Aquarium Soil (which softens and buffers the water) and the RO water, meant that my pH plummeted to 6.0 very quickly, which was beginning to become a stretch even for zebra danios.

Secondly, I had overlooked the fact the if you use RO water you must replace the minerals lost in the filtration process with a mineral supplement. I didn't do this to begin with, and my fish began to fail. The problem is that the lack of minerals adversely affects their osmoregulation, thus allowing minerals and salts to leach from the fish through their gills and bodies.

As soon as I noted all of this, I resolved to stop doing RO water changes, and gradually phased them out over a few days by alternating RO jugs with unfiltered tap water so as not to shock the fish. I saw an immediate improvement in my fish and in the pH level. The gH level also improved considerably as can be imagined.

Despite the London water being hard, my pH is still just under 7.0 and my gH is at acceptable levels. I had learned a lesson. Do not automatically assume London water is bad for your fish and be careful with that RO water. If you're going to use it, stir in a mineral supplement (such as Seachem Equilibrium).

Don't kill your fish with kindness by overfeeding

When your fish are new to your tank, it is understandable that you want to interact with them as much as possible. One of the ways of doing this is to feed them so you're able to watch them grabbing every little morsel they possibly can.

This can be very dangerous, especially if you are conducting fish-in cycling. The problem is that uneaten food decomposes and produces ammonia. This can be particularly problematic when fish-in cycling because the ammonia levels will already be high. I made a fundamental mistake in this regard when cycling my experimental 40-litre tank. Caught in fish-in cycling hell, my "suicide squad" Danios had taken to hugging the substrate lethargically and hiding behind plants because the ammonia and nitrite levels were so high. Desperate to make sure they were all right and they were accounted for, I would keep feeding them so they would swim to the surface and I could count them. Of course, this only exacerbated the problem.

I talked all this through with the manager at Maidenhead Aquatics in Morden, who to help me avoid killing my fish with kindness recommended I have the nerve during cycling to feed my Danios only once every other day, and that I skim any residue from the surface with a net after two minutes.

It nearly killed me to feed my fish only once every other day, especially as that made it almost impossible to inspect and account for my fish, but in fact I was being kind. Danios, they say, can last a fortnight without food[17], and they are opportunistic feeders. A feed every other day wouldn't harm them for a week or two while my tank was cycling.

---

17   I haven't tried starving my Danios for a fortnight myself, so I can't speak from experience.

Once my tank had cycled, I reverted to a more normal feeding regimen. I'll be honest and say that I suspect I still overfeed my fish a little, but it is not translating into high ammonia levels (about 0ppm). A specimen daily feeding regimen for my experimental 40-litre tank is as follows:

Figure 10: Daily feeding regimen for moderately-stocked 40-litre tank

Time	Feed
09:00	Two small pinches of fish flakes, to be eaten within two minutes
09:00	One pinch of catfish pellets
14:00	Two small pinches of fish flakes, to be eaten within two minutes
18:00 (Day One)	One third of a frozen cube of daphnia, melted down and mixed with a cup of tank water
18:00 (Day Two)	Three small pinches of fish flakes, to be eaten within two minutes
Lights Out	One pinch of catfish pellets

One dilemma I have is that while fishless cycling I got into the habit of skimming the residue from the top of the tank with a net after two minutes. I liked doing this because it made me feel I was doing the best by the fish, but I am aware that I now have catfish and Amano shrimp in my tank it is necessary to allow some residue to sink to the bottom so they can scavenge. I still have not made up my mind where the balance lies here.

Eventually, through a process of trial and error, you come to realise what the proper quantities of food are for your fish and you act accordingly. Whenever you buy more fish stock, however, the game changes again. How much extra food do you need to feed your additional numbers? It is, of course, a question of past experience and trial and error again. The key is, I think, only to give your fish enough fish flakes as they can eat in two minutes. The trouble is, of course, this rule of thumb doesn't necessarily work when you are feeding Corydoras catfish pellets, where the fish like the pellets to soften and to graze on them over time.

While you are adjusting to your new feeding quantities be sure to vacuum the substrate regularly to remove detritus, and also to test your water for ammonia and nitrite levels every day. It's ultimately a question of common sense.

Which leads me to my final thought on this topic: feeding fish is as much an art as a science. You have to practise, take notes, observe and correct your mistakes, and with time you will learn how to do it well.

On balance, less is more. For instance, whenever I feel I am overfeeding my fish I sometimes leave out their 14:00 feed, or cut out their daphnia, which tends to cloud over the tank and get everywhere even with only one third of a cube. Keep practising and you will get there. But continue vacuuming and water testing, and cut down a little if ammonia levels start to rise.

Use common sense when it comes to water changes

When I was in the midst of fish-in cycling hell, I reached out to numerous aquarists for advice about what to do. I got all sorts of advice, very little of it consistent. It got very confusing and I became deeply frustrated. Here is a summary of some of the different types of water changing advice I got.

Change your water:

- 25% every day

- 30% every day

- 50% every other day

- 50% every day

- Not at all for seven days while you try for a "bacterial bloom".

What was I to make of all this? I soon realised I was going to have to figure it out for myself and come to a practical, common sense view.

I started off with a few basic principles:

- In the normal course of events, when a tank has cycled, 25% of the water should be changed once a week. I conduct a slightly more reserved approach of changing 20% of the water twice a week[18]

- High ammonia and nitrite levels when a tank is fish-in cycling demand drastic action

- In the normal course of events water should be changed as little as reasonably possible, because pH, gH, kH, phosphate and temperature variations might distress the fish

- Tapsafe or another dechlorinator should always be used when changing water, which adds to the amount of chemicals in the tank

- Mineral supplements should be added when using RO water otherwise the fish may suffer.

---

18   Diana Walstad in her book *The Ecology of the Planted Aquarium* argues that in a well-balanced planted aquarium water changes might only be needed as little as once every six months (see below).

In the light of that, and given the distress my fish were in during cycling, I decided that I would change 25% of the water every day until cycling was complete. I would not use RO water but would use water direct from the tap even though we lived in London where the water was hard. This was an arduous task, and it took three weeks, but it was a labour of love and it seemed to work. My fish survived.

So, you should not overdo the water changes for the reasons given above, but there comes a time for emergency measures. Use your common sense, and you will get the balance right.

Don't panic if your aquarium soil buffers your pH

When I was cycling my experimental 40-litre tank, I was shocked to see that my pH plummeted to about 6.0. There were a number of reasons for this, including my use of RO water, my overfeeding the fish and the inevitable spike in ammonia and nitrite levels; but one of them was that I had used Tropica Aquarium Soil as my substrate. This has the deliberate effect of softening water and buffering pH, and according to the manufacturers the effect wears off over time, usually in about three months.

One of the problems with having a pH as low as 6.0, apart from it putting stress on the fish, is that nitrifying *Nitrosomonas* and *Nitrobacter* bacteria grow more slowly so that cycling takes longer. It was important therefore for me to increase my pH, and I aimed for a pH of 6.8–7.0. It was important to up the pH in gradations, because a sudden jump in pH might otherwise shock the fish.

I was so worried about my pH level and the consequent delay in cycling that I chose to use chemical intervention to bring my pH to 7.0. I bought a product called Neutral Regulator from Seachem, a highly regarded manufacturer, which explained that it would bring the tank to 7.0 in either direction. It also claimed to dechlorinate and to "detoxify" (rather than "remove") ammonia.[19]

After three careful doses of Neutral Regulator my pH reached about 6.8, and I stuck at that.

So, do not panic if your pH plummets. On the other hand, there's no room for complacency: you must do something about it, and do not be afraid to use reasonable and proportionate chemical interventions to bring your pH to 7.0, or thereabouts. If used judiciously, there are good products out there that can help you do it.

Don't over-use chemicals

Every time you use Tapsafe you are filling your tank with chemicals, so potentially polluting it. Of course, all aquarium products should be designed and

---

19 I was less happy with this ammonia detoxification facility because I wanted my ammonia to come down to zero through nitrifying bacteria and not through chemical intervention.

manufactured with the fish in mind, so these chemicals should not harm them. Nevertheless, chemicals are chemicals. Within reason, the more chemical-free the water the better.

It is almost impossible not to add some chemicals to a tank, especially when carrying out responsible water changes.

Here, for instance, is a list of the chemicals I add to my 40-litre tank every time I carry out a 20% water change twice a week:

Figure 11: Chemicals added to 40-litre tank on 20% water change twice weekly[20]

Product	Dose
Tapsafe	2ml
Neutral Regulator	1/4 teaspoon
Dr Tim's First Defense	2ml
Tropica Premium Nutrition	2 squirts
Fluval Biological Enhancer	5ml

That's as much as I would want to put into my tank. Obviously, if your fish develop diseases they must be treated and further chemicals will be necessary, remembering that some disease treatments may have adverse consequences for your filter media. Otherwise, measure out everything carefully and exactly, and don't overdo it!

Don't be afraid to plant your tank heavily

Unless you are deliberately opting for a cichlid biotope, I have never understood why some people do not want to plant their tanks heavily. To keep your fast growers in trim all that is needed is ten minutes' pruning and "gardening" once a fortnight.

I think some people are put off by the difficulty levels attached to maintaining challenging Aquascapes with difficult plants. But it's not necessary to plant up your aquarium with difficult plants, and it's not inevitable that you need to inject CO_2 into your well-planted tank. Within reason, all you need is appropriate substrate, bright lighting and an appropriate dose of fertiliser twice a week.

When I established my experimental 40-litre tank, I planted it up as heavily as I dared, but I exclusively chose easy growers. Within six weeks my tank looked mature and my plants were thriving. As has previously been mentioned, those who

---

20 Always carefully read and comply with manufacturer's instructions when using aquarium chemicals and other aquarium products.

read Diana Walstad's *Ecology of the Planted Aquarium* quickly come to realise the benefits of a well-planted aquarium as it strives for water quality balance.

Have the patience to do fishless cycling

Fishless cycling is easy: it just requires a bottle of ammonia and some fish flakes. But it needs one other factor: patience. Sadly, when it comes to establishing a new aquarium, patience often seems in short supply. Many people, when they buy their fish tank, want to put fish in immediately. Some retailers tell them to wait a week and then add some fish. The trouble with that is cycling will not start until there is an ammonia source. When the fish arrive, the fish themselves and the fish food remnants create an ammonia source and – slowly at first – the nitrifying bacteria can begin to grow.

This cycling process can take between two to twelve weeks, although it can be greatly shortened by the addition of live bacteria such as Dr Tim's One and Only. That's between two and twelve weeks when both fish and fishkeeper suffer: the fish because they are forced to live in water of very poor quality high in ammonia and nitrite; and the fishkeeper because, if he loves his fish, he will wake up every morning in a panic wondering have the fish survived the night, and almost inevitably succumb to carrying out an aggressive water changing regime.

If patience is the problem, perhaps because a loving parent cannot bear that their eight year old child has a tank but no fish for eight weeks, then consider this. Maybe that eight year old child gets a black molly and quickly falls in love with it. But fish-in cycling wreaks its havoc, and one morning after four weeks, the child comes down to breakfast to find his or her beloved black molly floating dead on the surface having succumbed to brown gill disease caused by ammonia and nitrite poisoning. What will the child do then? Better to have explained at the outset that, if the child wanted healthy fish that he or she could enjoy for years, he or she would need to wait for a month or so while the tank cycled. Enjoy the plants. Make a game of the chemistry and the water testing. Just don't buy fish until the tank has cycled.

And if that is not enough to persuade you, then Appendix 2 sets out a legal argument that strongly advances the contention that in many circumstances fish-in cycling is illegal in England and Wales under the Animal Welfare Act 2006.

Do yourself a favour and exercise patience. Grab that ammonia bottle, carry out fishless cycling, and let your fish be happy!

Give the bacteria a chance

When I had my community tank as a teenager in the 1980s, freshwater fishkeepers typically did not understand about the nitrogen cycle or nitrifying bacteria.

So the first time I advertently carried out a tank cycling was when I cycled my experimental 40-litre tank. I understood that *Nitrosomonas* bacteria consumed ammonia and converted it to nitrite, and that *Nitrobacter* bacteria consumed nitrite and converted it to much less harmful nitrate. And I understood that these bacteria multiply very slowly at first so that ammonia peaks, and then nitrite peaks, before eventually falling once the *Nitrosomonas* and *Nitrobacter* had established.

But there were some things I did not then understand, and learned by trial and error:

- Bacteria will not grow without an ammonia source, so you need to introduce either fish flakes, bottled ammonia (or a dead shrimp) or fish before the cycling process can begin. The point is, some people fill their tank with water and leave it empty for a week or so in the hopes the filter will mature. This is dead time: while it is important to let the tank settle for a couple of days before adding fish, the bacteria will not grow during this period. If you carry out fishless cycling you can add ammonia drops on day one.

- Bacteria do not like a low pH. Make sure the pH is 7.0 or above during the fishless cycling process.

- Bacteria do not like a low gH or kH. Add mineral supplements if necessary.

- Bacteria like a higher temperature. Raise the temperature to 30°C when fishless cycling to encourage faster cycling.

- When you buy your filter, buy the highest quality you can afford. Bacteria grow in the biological and other media in the filter, but if the filter breaks down (or is substandard) and you cannot source an identical filter, you may not be able to swop in the old filter's media. If this happens, you have to use new media and cycling must start over again from scratch. This happened to me when the first filter I bought was found to be substandard and I had to buy a new internal Fluval U2. This process delayed my cycling by a month.

- Add in substrate from a fully cycled tank.

- Acquire cycled filter media from a fully cycled tank and add it to your new filter.

- Don't allow excessively high spikes of ammonia or nitrite, because this can delay bacterial growth and so cycling.

The most controlled way to grow bacteria is when carrying out fishless cycling. It is then possible to manipulate the parameters of water quality and temperature without worrying about fish. Buy a bottle of ammonia and leave the fish out of it for the time being. The bacteria might thank you by growing more quickly than you might imagine.

Bacterial blooms: too good to be true?

When I was desperately seeking advice about what I should do about my fish-in cycling dilemma, one experienced aquarist told me I should stop water changing for a week and stop feeding the fish for five days and let the ammonia and nitrite levels rise until I generated a "bacterial bloom". The theory was that the bacteria in the bloom would almost immediately reduce the ammonia and nitrite levels to zero and the tank would then be fully cycled.

I tried this for five days (until my nerves couldn't stand it any more), but there was no sign of a bacterial bloom. Not even the beginnings of one. I began to wonder was this notion of a bacterial bloom too good to be true, and I began to do some research. The first thing to note was that none of the textbooks mentioned it. The second thing was that I found an abstract from an academic research paper by microbiologist Dr Tim Hovanec that suggested that nitrifying bacteria grew too slowly on the whole to render a bacterial bloom generally viable.

Apart from anything else, subjecting your "suicide squad" fish to a week of disastrous water quality without water changes is immensely cruel, especially if, as seems likely on the available evidence, a bacterial bloom is unlikely to occur.

Whether or not bacterial blooms are capable of occurring, the answer is a simple (and by now predictable) one. Exercise patience and conduct fishless cycling!

Don't overstock your tank

It is very tempting to cram as many fish as you can into your tank. When stocking, make sure you do your calculations carefully (e.g. one centimetre of adult fish per litre of water when using an internal filter). There are various methods you can use to increase stocking density such as using a pump and air stone to increase aeration and a wavemaker to improve water flow through the tank. But don't overdo it: you want a happy community, not the ichthyological equivalent of the Black Hole of Calcutta.

Have lots of shrimp

Shrimp cost basically zero on the fish-per-litre scale, partly because of the way they scavenge for detritus in your tank. The crude rule of thumb is one shrimp per five litres of water, and they prefer shoaling to being loners. So I have five Amano shrimp in my experimental 40-litre tank. In my new 240-litre tank I will have ten Amano shrimp and ten red cherry shrimp.

For those of you in doubt: have you ever considered a shrimp closely? Not only are they the most magnificent algae and tank cleaners, they are also the most beautiful and characterful invertebrates. And their habit of moulting their exoskeleton is highly endearing: I always feel for their naked vulnerability when they are skulking in the shadows while their next exoskeleton is hardening.

When stocking your tank, don't forget the shrimp!

Don't forget the zebra danio

Many people use zebra danios as workhorses, or "suicide squads", during the cycling process, but then forget about them, writing them off as so everyday and hardy as to present no challenge and be hardly worth bothering about.

I am not going to reiterate here how wonderful I think the zebra danio is. Just refer back to Chapters 7 and 9. When stocking your tank, don't forget the humble zebra danio. Make a home for a shoal in your tank, and it will reward you with character a thousand-fold.

Read as many textbooks as you can get your hands on

Knowledge is power. It is also a safety net. Read all the textbooks you can get your hands on, and don't be snobbish. For instance, the Dummies Series has an excellent book on keeping tropical freshwater fish. And don't forget to read the magazines either. *Practical Fishkeeping* and *Tropical Fish Hobbyist* are both excellent reads. If you are wondering where to start, the select bibliography at the end of this book might help.

Choose as big a tank as you can afford
and can fit into your house

When I bought my experimental 40-litre tank, I deliberately bought small precisely because it was an experiment and I wasn't sure that I would rekindle the fishkeeping flame. When the bug bit, I immediately started planning for a bigger tank. I settled on a Fluval New Roma 240-litre because it was the biggest tank that would reasonably fit into our house. Moreover, it was long and sleek and not too wide. If you skimp on a tank, as you grow into the hobby you will only become frustrated because you will want to keep buying specimens (perhaps spontaneously – who can resist a trip to the fish store?) and run the risk of overstocking.

Once you have bought a tank, to buy a larger one will either require space for a second tank, or you will need to break down the first tank and find a home for your fish while you are cycling the second. So get the biggest tank you reasonably can first up – and save yourself a lot of frustration.

Buy the best equipment you can

When I bought my experimental 40-litre tank I bought a cheap filter. This was a big mistake. As I have described elsewhere in this book, it did not generate sufficient water flow for my tank, and its design did not encourage the rapid growth of nitrifying bacteria. Worse, fish could wriggle their way into the filter, with fatal results. I soon had to buy a more adequate Fluval U2 replacement filter, so incurring extra expense and delaying my tank cycling by a month.

I learnt a huge lesson from this. Always buy the best kit you can for your aquarium, especially when it comes to "heartbeat" equipment such as filters and heaters.

Consider an experimental tank

If you're not sure about the hobby, or your skills are rusty and you want to make sure you still have fishy fingers, why not invest in a small experimental tank. I did exactly that and I never regretted it. The things I learned from six months managing an experimental tank set me in excellent stead for buying my 240-litre tank.

You can achieve a healthy balance between Aquascaping and fishkeeping

In Chapter 10, I argue that aquarium management is a compromise between planted Aquascaping and practical fishkeeping. Experts who maintain incredibly lush Aquascapes sometimes put the Aquascape first and the fish second. On the other hand, a cichlid enthusiast might have a rocky biotope with practically no planting at all.

Don't be put off by either of these extremes: there is a happy compromise. You can have a beautiful and heavily planted tank in which a community of contented fish thrive (and if you choose the right species of fish and plants, the plants won't be eaten).

Stock your tank slowly

Once your tank has cycled it's tempting to buy out the store and dump a zillion fish into your tank all at once. Don't do it. As you add stock you will have a predictable, but hopefully small, ammonia and nitrite spike.

I made this mistake with my 40-litre experimental tank when, before the tank had fully cycled, I impatiently added five new Danios to my initial population of three, primarily because I wanted to make sure they quickly became a coherent shoal. I paid the price in high ammonia and nitrite levels and the necessity for aggressive and frequent water changes. Make a plan to add a few fish at a time and stick to it.

Don't buy spontaneously

Let's face it, we've all succumbed to the temptation to reach for our wallet when we see a beautiful new fish at the fish store. There's a certain joy in the spontaneous buy. But don't do it. Plan. Always plan. Plan meticulously. Research the fish, learn about its adult length, feeding habits, territoriality, inter-species behaviour patterns. Consider the integrity of your biotope, do your centimetre of fish per litre calculations. Go home and gaze at your tank and calmly and dispassionately come to a view about whether the fish in question is really the right buy. Make a commitment *never* to succumb to a spontaneous buy. Do it now.

Research what you put in your tank

I once spontaneously bought some liquid carbon enhancer in the hopes of compromising on CO_2 injection. When I got home I read the ingredients and realised it included a poison that had been banned for use by the NHS. This was confirmed to me when I made enquiries of the *UK Aquatic Plant Society* Forum. Luckily, I hadn't yet squirted the enhancer into the tank. It got thrown in the bin pretty quickly. Always research what you're putting into your tank. You never know what's in those bottles!

Don't panic when moving house with a fish tank

There can be few things that bring aquarists out in a cold sweat more than the thought of breaking an aquarium down when they move house.

Rule 1: "Don't Panic." It's basically just the inverse of setting up a tank.

Rule 2: Try to leave a day clear in between moving in and moving out to allow you to break down the aquarium in peace and quiet. If you try to do it on the day of the move, there will be so much going on that you will get flustered and be in the way.

Rule 3: Under no circumstances try to lift or otherwise move the aquarium with any water or substrate in it.

Rule 4: Try to enlist the assistance of a friend who knows something about fishkeeping to help.

For the purposes of this discussion, I am assuming that you are moving not too far. If the move requires travel of more than a few hours then seek help from your fish store. In fact, you should ask for your fish store's advice when you're conducting a manoeuvre like this in any event. You might be surprised at how they might be able to help out.

I also assume that you have scoped out the placement of your tank in your new house in an appropriate place and that the floor is sufficiently load-bearing and the electrics are safe, etc.

Beyond that, you will need a few extra items:

- Three large buckets with sealable lids

- Plastic bags and rubber bands from the fish store sufficient to bag your fish stock responsibly

- Large insulating freezer bags.

A tank breakdown and reassembly protocol might be as follows:

- Bag the fish and shrimp ensuring there is plenty of air in the bag.

- Fill a large bucket with old tank water and float the fish bags in it. Seal the lid so the fish are in darkness (they will be calmer that way). Try to surround the fish bags with insulating material. Another possibility is to wedge the fish bags into insulating freezer bags and then put them in the bucket with the sealable lid.

- Turn off the filter and the heater and leave the heater in the tank to cool down for twenty minutes.

- Place the filter media in the bucket of old tank water so it does not dry out.

- Carefully uproot the plants and bag them with a little water so they don't dry out. Seal the plants in the second bucket.

- Syphon off the remaining tank water. If you are able, keep as much of it as you reasonably can.

- Remove the substrate and rocks from the tank and place in the third bucket with some water to ensure it doesn't dry out (the substrate houses nitrifying bacteria, too).

- Move the cabinet/stand, tank, filter, heater, three buckets and all your other equipment to the new house as quickly as possible. Never carry anything that is too heavy or which might otherwise injure you.

- Set up the tank in its new position in the new house as you would with a new tank, making sure that the fish are safe, and that the substrate, filter media and plants do not dry out.

- Use as much of your old tank water as you have kept to fill the tank.

- Using Tapsafe, heat some additional new water to the extent required to heat the aquarium to the necessary temperature.

- Add an appropriate dose of an effective biological enhancer and fish destressing solution, if required.

- In a perfect world you would let the tank settle overnight, but it is not a perfect world and the fish are in bags. Put the fish in the tank as quickly as possible, while not forgetting to float the bags on the surface to adjust the temperature of the in-bag water and avoid shocking the fish.

- You will not need to cycle the tank as long as the filter media and substrate have been kept in your old tank water and have not dried out.

The bottom line is planning. Plan your move and tank breakdown and reassembly meticulously and give yourself time and things should go smoothly. Ideally, do a "dry-run" walk through before carrying out the operation in earnest. Good luck!

Join the UK Aquatic Plant Society

The UK Aquatic Plant Society (UKAPS) was founded some years ago by George Farmer, the renowned Aquascaper. It is an online forum that is knowledgeable, friendly and accessible. I have asked many questions on the Forum, even ones I was pretty sure I knew the answer to, because there is always another perspective or piece of advice. The Society has many Forum topics, from Aquascaping, to CO_2 injection, to invertebrates, and it is free to join. It is a must for any serious aquarist.

Don't be afraid to ask questions – even dumb ones

In a similar vein, don't be afraid to ask any reasonable question you want. No question is too basic or dumb, and most aquarists, whether on the UKAPS Forum or in the fish store, will be only too happy to answer them.

Enjoy your hobby and have a beer

Once all the cycling, fish stocking, paranoia and stress is done, it's time to remember what it's all about and sit back with a beer and enjoy the watery world you have created. Perhaps you might consider listening to *Carnival of the Animals* and gazing at a 17th-century Dutch study of fish while you do so.

Congratulations! You've made it.

13

Conclusion

It was James Cromwell who said: "Pets are humanizers. They remind us we have an obligation and responsibility to preserve and nurture and care for all life."

In this book I have argued that tropical freshwater fish are inherently valuable in their own right. They have the same rights as other pet animals, and deserve to be treated with compassion and respect. Whether or not those rights arise by operation of legal norms, or through natural law, or simply by means of more constrained utilitarian measures like primary legislation such as The Animal Welfare Act 2006 (or the simple but powerful argument that the world is a better place and we feel better about ourselves with healthy, happy, tropical freshwater fish) is in my view a moot point. I would argue, however, that animals adopted as pets, including freshwater tropical fish kept in aquariums, have a higher status in the context of rights than, say livestock or game animals.

There is a growing international trend to recognize that vertebrates, including of course teleost fish, are sentient and can feel pleasure, pain and fear. At the time of writing the Government in England and Wales had just presented the Animal Welfare (Sentience) Bill which enshrines the notion of vertebrate sentience in English law. When you buy a pet, you make a commitment to look after it. Now, when you buy a fish as a pet, the concept of animal sentience in conjunction with the obligations of pet-owners under the Animal Welfare Act, means, I think, that you must avoid subjecting it to pain, fear and suffering. I would argue further that pet-owning fishkeepers have a higher obligation to keep their fish "happy". At the end of the day, why buy a fish tank for pets if you want to stock your tank full of distressed, unhappy fish? What sort of fishkeeper would you be?

I would therefore argue that foremost amongst the rights of pets, including tropical freshwater fish, is for them to be treated humanely and without suffering. As is evident, one of the themes of this book has been my distaste for fish-in cycling. It seems to me that fish-in cycling is in most instances a product of the lazy trait of failing to put patience into gear. To my mind fish-in cycling is regularly close to an abomination and may well often comprise offences in England and Wales under Ss 4 and 9 of the Animal Welfare Act (See Appendix 2). Fish-in cycling should be discouraged by everyone.

Equally, the fact that many tropical fish have the status of Least Concern on the IUCN Red List does not necessarily mean we can be complacent. It may mean, for instance, that captive breeding and aquarium biotopes have rendered the conservation of such species a relative success. It may also mean that, as in the case of *Danio rerio*, the population is declining notwithstanding its current Least Concern status, so that if we are not careful and wild capture continues and habitat loss increases, it may not be long before species such as *Danio rerio* become more endangered. That would be a shame to say the least. Finally, many popular tropical fish species are data deficient or not recorded on the Red List so we are complacent at our peril.

It was George Eliot who said: "Animals are such agreeable friends – they ask no questions, they pass no criticisms." In that context, who can argue that tropical freshwater fish are not the perfect pet? They give us colour and character, they award us purpose, and they lead us to a fascinating learning curve of scientific technicalities, know-how and equipment.

Beyond that, our fish surprise us. When I took up fishkeeping again, I was not expecting I would fall in love with that most humble, compliant and hardy of fish, the zebra danio. But fall in love with it I did. What's not to be fascinated about by this little minnow fish? It has been into space. It has saved lives through biomedical research. Its horizontal bands shimmer brightly like agate and silver. And it has led me through the gateway to a brave new world of glowlight danios, blue danios, gold ring danios and panther danios, to name but a few. Who would have thought it? The workhorse of the fish-in cycling "suicide squads" has led me to set up a biotope tank stocked almost exclusively by Danios.

I felt like C.S. Lewis – *Surprised by Joy*. As he wrote in that work: "Who can describe beauty? The reader may smile at this as the far-off echo of a precocious calf love, but he will be wrong. There are beauties so unambiguous that they need no lens of that kind to reveal them; they are visible even to the careless and objective eyes of a child."

Which leads me to my final point. For good or ill, as may be discernible from some of my other observations in this book, I believe in God. As such, I know that tropical freshwater fish are intrinsically valuable not only because they may have rights conferred under law. They are also a part of God's Creation and glorify God through the very fact they are fish and through their role as our pets. As a result, they demand our compassion, respect and safeguarding.

May God bless all aquarists in that endeavour. And God bless our tropical fish.

14

Appendices

Appendix 1: Robert's 240-litre tank list (for fishless cycling)

Item	Number	Price
NEW Fluval Roma 240-litre tank and matching walnut cabinet	1	TBC
Fluval 407 Filter. Please swap out the included F307 filter with an F407	1 (included, but swap out 307 for 407)	Within tank cost plus excess
Heater	1 (included)	Within tank cost
Bluetooth LED lighting system (14.5W)	1 (included)	Within tank cost
Substrate. Tropica aquarium soil - both plant and Corydoras friendly	As required (4 large bags)?	TBC
Rocks and bogwood hardscape	Several. Require midground rocks and background bogwood	TBC
Plants (see separate Plant List at End)	Sufficient to heavily plant 250 litre tank	TBC
Dr Tim's One and Only for 250 litres		TBC
Ammonia (for fishless cycling)		TBC
First Defense for 250 L		TBC
Wavemaker (Fluval circulation pump)	0	N/A
2D background	May leave back clear?	TBC

Figure 12: Proposed purchases for possible 240-litre tank

I plan to have a Danio-specialist tank. Danios I might want to include – although obviously I cannot include all – are any of glowlight danios (*Danio choprai*), zebra danios (*Danio rerio*), orange-finned danios (*Danio ryathil*), blue danios (*Danio kerri*), gold ring danios (*Danio tinwini*) and panther danios (*Danio aesculapii*). All advice and suggestions greatly appreciated. Because this will be a Danio tank, I will look for the pH to be about 6.8–7.0, and I will maintain water temperature at 24°C. Substrate, rocks and wood will need to reflect this, as will planting. I aim to have a heavily planted tank, so substrate will also need to reflect that. I intend for a small school of bronze corys (*Corydoras aenous*) and pepper corys (*Corydoras paleatus*) or leopard corys (*Corydoras leopardus*) so aquarium soil or sand will probably be the best substrate. (Will these bronze and leopard corys school together?)

Plants

I intend my Aquascape to be heavily planted, and hopefully you can advise me about how many of each of these specimens I need for a heavily planted tank. Rather than using a CO_2 injector I will probably fertilise the tank with Tropica Premium/Specialist Nutrition.

Ideally my plants would be bundled into three labelled containers, one each for foreground/carpeting plants, midground plants and background plants. I might also try out a bit of moss for the wood if you can supply some appropriate glue.

In terms of composition, I am looking for two species of foreground plants, three species (one red) of midground plants, and two species of background plants (one cabomba-like, one more broad-leaved) to form a "curtain" along the rear of the tank.

Figure 13: Specimen selection of plants for proposed 240-litre tank.

Foreground/Carpeting	Moss
Hellanthium tenellum "Green" Micranthemum "Monte Carlo" Hemianthus callitrichoides "Cuba"	One type of moss to glue to the rocks. E.g. Taxyphillum "Spikey".
Midground	**Background**
Cryptocoryne wendtii "Green" Cryptocoryne X willistii Pogostemon erectus	Green cabomba caroliniana Amazon sword (Echinodorus "blehrae") Bacopa caroliniana Hygrophilia "siamensis 53B" Limnophilia hippuroides

Appendix 2: The illegality of fish-in cycling under the Animal Welfare Act 2006

Background

When you establish a new aquarium to house tropical freshwater fish, it may develop something called "New Tank Syndrome" (NTS). NTS occurs as follows. Many people put fish in their tank immediately, and these fish (and the remnants of the fish food they are fed) excrete ammonia (NH_3), which is extremely harmful to fish at levels exceeding 0.02ppm.

Typically, over time, a tank "cycles", thus preventing NTS. But it takes time – maybe as much as twelve weeks – to cycle a tank. When a tank cycles, the filter media in the tank's filter grows *Nitrosomonas* bacteria, which convert the harmful ammonia into (almost equally as harmful) nitrite (NO_2). And then the filter grows *Nitrobacter* bacteria[21], which convert the nitrite to much less harmful nitrate (NO₃). Once this occurs, the tank is said to be "cycled" and ammonia and nitrite levels typically revert to near zero.

There are two main ways to cycle a tank. The first is to introduce fish immediately so that the ammonia they produce can kick-start the cycling process. This is called "fish-in cycling". The second is not to introduce fish, but to plant the fish tank up with plants and introduce an artificial ammonia source such as ammonia from a bottle and/or fish flakes to kick start the cycle. This is called "fishless cycling". Some people do not like fishless cycling because it means, perhaps, that they may have to wait for up to twelve weeks (often less) before introducing a stock of fish.

When conducting fish-in cycling it is important to carry out regular daily 25% water changes. Even with this regimen, ammonia and nitrite levels might spike at 2ppm–4ppm each. This causes the fish needlessly to suffer. Ammonia and nitrite poisoning will typically cause fish to gasp at the surface, or cling to the substrate in lethargy, or develop an ailment called brown gill disease which adversely affects the ability of their blood to oxygenate and may destroy their gills. Ultimately death may ensue. They will at the least certainly suffer.

In the vast majority of cases fish-in cycling is completely unnecessary. All that is needed is a modicum of patience with fishless cycling and fish stocks can be added once cycling is completed thus avoiding suffering. It is possible to envisage circumstances where fish-in cycling is unavoidable, however. One example might

---

21   There are disputes about the precise identification of the bacteria that are responsible for tank cycling because arguably *Nitrosomonas* and *Nitrobacter* bacteria are only found in water and sewage treatment plants where the ammonia and nitrite levels are much higher.

be where a filter breaks down and for some reason a new identical filter cannot be sourced so the old filter media (complete with cycled bacteria) cannot be swopped in. Subject to that sort of eventuality, however, there is a very strong argument that fish-in cycling is completely unnecessary. Fishless cycling is almost always a viable alternative. Moreover, oftentimes people choose fish-in cycling over fishless cycling quite deliberately and in full knowledge of what will occur.

The Animal Welfare Act 2006 (the "Act")

The Act establishes a number of offences around the treatment of animals. For these purposes, by S1 the definition of "animal" includes any vertebrate. So, it includes tropical freshwater fish, but oddly not Amano shrimp (*Caridina multidentata*) or red cherry shrimp (*Neocaridina davidi*), etc. which might also reside in a tropical tank, because they are invertebrates[22].

Two key definitions:

Protected animals

S1 an animal is a "protected animal" for the purposes of this Act if:

(a) it is of a kind which is commonly domesticated in the British Islands,

(b) it is under the control of man whether on a permanent or temporary basis, or

(c) it is not living in a wild state.

This obviously therefore includes tropical freshwater fish in a tank.

Persons responsible for an animal

S3 (1) In this Act, references to a person responsible for an animal are to a person responsible for an animal whether on a permanent or temporary basis.

---

22   There is an animated debate about the extent to which shrimp and invertebrates generally should be subject to the Animal Welfare Act 2006. The Act contemplates the extension of its protection to other types of animals other than vertebrates if it can be proven that they are capable of experiencing pain. It is interesting to note that at the time of writing the Government's Animal Welfare (Sentience) Bill does not include cephalopods and decapods in the definition of "Animal" for its purposes; and it has been criticised in this regard. The British Veterinary Association (in its policy position paper on the recognition of animals as sentient beings), states:

Section 1 of the Animal Welfare Act 2006 provides a useful starting point for considering which animals would be considered sentient under the law. However, that basis is insufficient as it fails to recognise and protect the sentience of cephalopods, decapods and pre-natal animal forms. Any future legislation should incorporate such recognition and protection, over and above the basis provided by the Animal Welfare Act 2006. The Global Animal Law Project... states that scientific research confirms that all vertebrates (fish, amphibians, reptiles, birds and mammals) are sentient animals and indicates sentience in some invertebrates. Evidence indicates that cephalopods (e.g. octopus, squid) and decapods (e.g. lobsters, crabs [and shrimp]) are sentient, and are capable of experiencing pain and distress... Already the Animals (Scientific Procedures) Act 1986 Amendment Regulations 2012 (administered by the Home Office), includes "any living cephalopod" and animals in their "foetal, larval or embryonic form" within the category of protected animals.

(2) In this Act, references to being responsible for an animal include being in charge of it.

(3) For the purposes of this Act, a person who owns an animal shall always be regarded as being a person who is responsible for it.

Therefore the owner of a fish tank will be responsible for it (unless they are under 16 in which case it will normally be his or her parent).

Offences

There appear to be two directly relevant offences under S4 and S9[23].

4 - Unnecessary suffering

(1) A person commits an offence if—

(a) an act of his, or a failure of his to act, causes an animal to suffer,

(b) he knew, or ought reasonably to have known, that the act, or failure to act, would have that effect or be likely to do so,

(c) the animal is a protected animal, and

(d) the suffering is unnecessary.

There is an almost unassailable argument that fish-in cycling would comprise an offence under S4.

9 - Duty of person responsible for animal to ensure welfare

(1) A person commits an offence if he does not take such steps as are reasonable in all the circumstances to ensure that the needs of an animal for which he is responsible are met to the extent required by good practice.

(2) For the purposes of this Act, an animal's needs shall be taken to include—

(a) its need for a suitable environment,

(b) its need for a suitable diet,

(c) its need to be able to exhibit normal behaviour patterns,

(d) any need it has to be housed with, or apart from, other animals, and

(e) its need to be protected from pain, suffering, injury and disease.

---

23   There are some other interesting, but not directly relevant, offences that might relate to tropical fish. Some people, for instance, like to "fight" their Siamese fighting fish (*Betta splendens*), and this may well now be an offence under S8 of the Act.

Again, the practice of fish-in cycling would seem to fall within the scope of the offence in S9.

Sentience

Arguably an animal cannot suffer if it cannot feel pain. The field of animal sentience is hotly debated and is, to an extent, controversial. Nevertheless, over the past twenty years or so a considerable body of evidence has developed that persuasively argues that fish are sentient and can feel pain; and this position has been adopted by the European Union and the RSPCA, amongst others. The EU AHAW Panel has declared[24] that:

> "The balance of the evidence indicates that some fish species[25] have the capacity to experience pain" and that... "Responses of fish, of some species and under certain situations, suggest that they are able to experience fear" and that... "There is scientific evidence to support the assumption that some fish species have brain structures potentially capable of experiencing pain and fear."

Professor Donald Broom, of the University of Cambridge, sums up the case for fish feeling pain:

> "There are some differences in sensory functioning between fish and mammals because fish live in water but the pain system of fish is very similar to that of birds and mammals. Fish have pain receptor cells, nociceptive neuronal pathways, specialized transmitter substances, electrophysiological responses to cuts, bruises and electric shocks, behavioural avoidance, learned avoidance of places where they had unpleasant experiences and processing systems in the brain which parallel those in birds and mammals. Hence at least some aspects of pain as we know it must be felt by fish."

In its Policy Paper on the Recognition of Animals as Sentient Beings, the British Veterinary Association recommends that the Government adopts a statutory definition of sentience:

> "There is growing scientific understanding of animal sentience, and of how to objectively assess animal interests, due to the growth of animal welfare science as a scientific discipline and to the growing number of universities, including veterinary schools, offering animal welfare courses. Government should ensure clarity by providing a definition of sentience. This will avoid confusion with terms and concepts that are closely associated with sentience and are often used interchangeably, but which may have mixed meanings such as awareness, cognition and consciousness. We propose the definition of sentience developed by the Global Animal Law Project: 'Sentience shall

---

24 General Approach to Fish Welfare and the Concept of Sentience in Fish.
25 The AHAW referred to "some fish species" because only a limited number of species was studied.

be understood to mean the capacity to have feelings, including pain and pleasure, and implies a level of conscious awareness."

It continues by supporting the contention that fish (and interestingly shrimp) should be determined to be sentient:

"The Global Animal Law Project, referred to above, states that scientific research confirms that all vertebrates (fish, amphibians, reptiles, birds and mammals) are sentient animals and indicates sentience in some invertebrates. Evidence indicates that cephalopods (e.g. octopus, squid) and decapods (e.g. lobsters, crabs) are sentient, and are capable of experiencing pain and distress. Already the Animals (Scientific Procedures) Act 1986 Amendment Regulations 2012 (administered by the Home Office), includes "any living cephalopod" and animals in their "foetal, larval or embryonic form" within the category of protected animals."

Moreover, fish sentience expert Dr Victoria Braithwaite states that it is likely that fish are capable of subjective emotion[26]:

"The presence of a limbic-like area in the fish forebrain, and evidence that fish change the way they view an aversive situation—electric shocks or novel objects—certainly seems to suggest fish have the capacity for subjective emotions. For sure, we have not found a definitive test to categorically show the presence of subjective emotion in fish, so we need to be cautious about how we interpret these results. But we have trouble getting such evidence for any non-human—in fact, we would probably struggle to do this for any human if we could not understand their language."

In this context, Dr Braithwaite concludes[27]:

"On balance then, fish have a capacity for some forms of consciousness, and so I conclude that they therefore have the mental capacity to feel pain. I suspect that what they experience will be different and simpler than the experiences we associate with pain and suffering, but I see no evidence to deny them these abilities, and quite a bit which argues that they will suffer from noxious stimuli."

At the time of writing, the British Government had, as part of its Animal Welfare Action Plan, just published its new Animal Welfare (Sentience) Bill, which acknowledges, amongst other things, that vertebrates are capable of experiencing pleasure, pain and fear and that the concept of sentience in animals should be overseen by an Animal Sentience Committee[28]. Beyond this, it is not really for this book to discuss this issue further. For those who are interested, I should

---

26   Braithwaite, Victoria. *Do Fish Feel Pain?* (pp. 105–106), OUP Oxford, Kindle Edition.
27   Ibid. (pp. 112–113).
28   Although the Bill has been criticised for not including cephalopods and decapods in the definition of "Animal" for these purposes.

perhaps add that this whole topic has been exhaustively addressed in the late Dr Victoria Braithwaite's excellent and accessible book *Do Fish Feel Pain?* and in Jonathan Balcolmbe's fine book *What a Fish Knows – The Inner Lives of our Underwater Cousins.*

Enforcement

In the case of an offence under S9, an inspector may issue an improvement notice. Under S18 of the Act theoretically an inspector could enter a tank-owner's premises and confiscate the tank. Under S30 a local authority in England or Wales may prosecute proceedings for any offences under the Act. Offences under S4 and S9 are dealt with summarily and the maximum penalty is an unlimited fine and/or six months' imprisonment[29].

Summary

From the above, it would seem there is a strong argument that the use of fish-in cycling comprises, in the vast majority of cases, offences under S4 and S9 of the Animal Welfare Act 2006.

As I understand it, the law is correct as at 13 May 2021.

Review

This opinion has been reviewed by Mr Rupert Butler, barrister-at-law at 3 Hare Court, Middle Temple, and by Harbottle & Lewis LLP.

---

29   The Animal Welfare (Sentencing) Bill contemplates increasing the maximum sentence for animal welfare offences to five years' imprisonment.

Appendix 3: Irish Times Amazon article (2021)

COP26 – Time to take The Amazon seriously

The European Green Deal commits the EU to achieving net zero CO_2 emissions by 2050. COP26, held in Glasgow in November 2021, is the latest step along the road of the Paris Climate Change Treaty.

In the meantime, world leaders met virtually on 22 April to discuss climate change, during which the US committed to cut carbon emissions by 50–52% below 2005 levels by 2030. On top of the EU's recent legal framework to cut carbon emissions by at least 55% by 2030, it looks like we are making progress.

Nevertheless, the world is in COP26's hands. Obviously much of the Conference's focus will be to scrutinize the viability of the Nations' roadmaps towards net zero, but there are also other things the Conference can do.

One is to focus on the plight of the Amazon. The Amazon is located mostly in Brazil and currently comprises about six million square kilometers of rainforest. It is currently being cut down at the rate of about 200,000 acres a day.

The effect this will have on biodiversity is obvious, but a big problem in terms of climate change is that trees store CO_2, of which the Amazon is estimated to capture about 400 billion tons. The release of this will have an important effect on greenhouse gasses and so the ability of the world to keep global mean temperature rise below 2°C, ideally to 1.5°C as envisioned by Paris.

There are other implications. There will almost certainly be a detrimental effect on weather systems, and we have already seen forest fires raging. There will be implications for soil erosion and question-marks over the long-term viability of cleared farmland.

Jair Bolsonaro, the President of Brazil, has consistently claimed that the Amazon is Brazil's sovereignty and the international community should not interfere. This was recently evidenced when in 2019 the G7 suggested a £16 million package to help combat Amazonian wildfires and Bolsonaro refused it. To be fair, Bolsonaro perhaps regarded the offer of such a parsimonious amount as an insult – what's £16 million in the context of saving the Amazon?

It is understood the US and Brazil have been conducting discussions for an Amazon Protection Agreement. But April's Earth Day Summit suggests they are stalemated. Bolsonaro has made clear Amazon conservation is dependent on financial contributions from other nations.

This moment gives future inspiration. Why not set up (under the auspices of UNESCO?) an International Amazon Protection Fund into which Europe and the G20 could contribute collectively, say, £5 billion a year towards Amazonian preservation and regeneration? Bolsonaro would be unlikely to scoff at such an amount.

There are arguments that Brazil could not be trusted with this money. But the *quid pro quo* should be that the cash is managed by a new international body, which should supervise Brazil's anti-deforestation efforts, much as a charity receiving a grant would be subject to impact, monitoring and evaluation assessments.

Brazil has other objections. Why should it halt its deforestation of the Amazon when the West has denuded its own forests? For Bolsonaro, the West's entreaties to stop felling the Amazon are just plain hypocrisy. On one level, it's hard to disagree. The West substantially developed its farming and industry around the felling of its own forests, so why should Brazil not do likewise?

The answer is that now we know what we are doing to the environment and the climate, whereas previously we did not; and now the Amazon and a few other forests comprise the last vestiges of global rainforest cover.

There is another complementary answer to this conundrum: the West can seek to put its money and its land where its mouth is and commence its own forest regeneration programme.

Forest cover in Ireland is estimated at 11%, one of the lowest in the EU. In some European countries proposals exist to increase forest cover by a substantial amount. In the UK, the Government has committed to planting 30,000 hectares of new trees per year between 2020–2050, so increasing the UK's forest cover (including Scotland) from 13% to 17%.

There is an argument that Ireland should do likewise, and an increase of Irish forest cover by just 1–2% would make a significant difference.

Donal Whelan, Technical Director of the Irish Tree Growers' Association, highlights Ireland's modest national planting target of just 8,000 hectares per annum (about 1% of current forest cover); however, less than one third of this is being achieved. Whelan is optimistic, however, that when a new strategy is developed these targets can be achieved or even exceeded.

These two initiatives might go a long way towards rescuing the Amazon. Perhaps Ireland could incentivize the EU to make these proposals at COP26 and persuade Brazil to take the Amazon seriously. At around the time of COP26, Ireland is scheduled to host the PEFC International General Assembly, the annual assembly of the world's largest forest certification scheme, giving Ireland a major profile on the world stage and potential to show real leadership.

It used to be the humourists' joke that a paper cut was a tree's final revenge. But that's no longer the case. Imagine the bittersweet revenge when all those billions of tonnes of previously sequestered carbon are released into the atmosphere to choke our planet. The Amazon is no joke. Next time you think about it, just realise how we might save it if we try.

Appendix 4: Early draft of Tropical Fish Hobbyist Magazine article

Bacterial Blooms and Suicide Squads

A returning aquarist's surprise at new techniques

By Robert Porter

Just under forty years ago – at the age of thirteen – I set up my first community tank. It was a resounding success, and I owned it successfully for four happy years until we moved house. I was an extremely keen aquarist, and even – at such a tender age – had a lengthy letter published in one of the then magazines of the moment, *The Aquarist and Pondkeeper*.

My tank then was quite eclectic and not at all ichthyologically coherent. I crammed everything in there from neon tetras (*Paracheirodon innesi*) to a red tailed black shark (*Labeo bicolor*) (that prowled territorially behind the filter) to dwarf gouramis (*Colisa lalia*) to a Siamese fighting fish (*Betta splendens*) and even a long-lived ram (*Microgeophagus ramirezi*). My favourites were two perky little bronze corys (*Corydoras aeneus*), full of character. As you can imagine, I had two filters on the go: a basic normally configured under-gravel, and an early adopter internal filter. It was an eccentric tank, but I loved it, and I adored my fish. But, as I say, I had to give up the hobby when we moved.

I was recently reminded of the beauty of tropical fish and aquariums when I happened to brose a copy of a leading tropical fishkeeping hobbyists' magazine, and I decided to jump in again immediately and buy myself a small 40-litre experimental tank as a precursor to getting something larger.

One of the problems with my old community tank was that, because it had an under-gravel filter, it was difficult to get plants to establish and thrive. With my new experimental aquarium I poured in substrate soil and delightedly planted the aquarium up with a whole series of hardy aquatic plants: vallisneria (*Vallisnaria americana*), an Amazon sword plant (*Echinodorus bleheri*), dragon flame

105

(*Alternanthera reineckii*) and the vigorous green cabomba (*Cabomba caroliniana*), amongst others. They all took quickly and are thriving to date.

Aside from this Aquascape triumph, I was shocked at what I have just learned. When I set up my community tank all those years ago, one of the fishkeeping bibles was a book by Derek McInerny and Geoffrey Gerard called *All About Tropical Fish* (1980). In it, there was plenty of mention about pH levels and CO_2, but nothing at all about ammonia and nitrite. Equally, thirty five years ago under-gravel filters were all the rage, while now they seem to be regarded with circumspection. It's obvious that the fishkeeping techniques in *All About Tropical Fish* are outdated, but, as I understand it, its fish descriptions remain some of the best.

Most recently, I devoured Jeremy Gay's *The Perfect Aquarium* (2005) and *The Aquarium Masterclass*, and realised that, rather than already knowing it all as I had thought, I had to start learning again from scratch.

This conviction was enhanced when I spoke at length to the knowledgeable aquarist who is the manager of the shop where I bought my tank. I don't remember having a case of "New Tank Syndrome" when I established my community tank all those years ago, and indeed I suspect I then introduced a wide variety of community fish only a few days after pouring water into it for the first time.

Now, at the manager's suggestion, I waited at least a week after filling my new experimental tank before introducing my first fish – a small shoal of zebra danios (*Danio rerio*). Diligently I tested my ammonia and nitrite levels daily and quickly became alarmed when they rose steadily (to 3ppm and 2ppm respectively) and the fish became lethargic.

I raced back to the manager for advice, and he reassured me that it wasn't on the whole too early to have introduced zebra danios, because these fish were what one might call a "suicide squad" which would kick start the growth of bacteria in my filter and so the ammonia/nitrite/nitrate cycle in my tank. This would provoke a "bacterial bloom", soon after which the daily levels would almost certainly settle down, and the levels would return to zero.

Although the suicide squad would become lethargic, zebra danios were extremely hardy, and they would almost certainly be alright in the pre-bacterial bloom adverse conditions for a good few days. The key was to have the nerve not to carry out daily tank changes, to stop feeding the danios for several days, and just trust that the bacterial bloom would occur.

Never do I remember biting my fingernails so hard than over the intervening three days. Each morning I inspected my tank, expecting fish to rise dead to the surface at any moment, but in that context this never happened.

A problem then intervened. It turned out that my filter – which had been supplied with my all-in-one tank – was almost certainly substandard for two reasons. First, the water flow through the filter was not powerful enough for it to be a really effective filter. And secondly (and most alarmingly) fish kept getting caught and killed in the filter and I lost three danios that way. There's an argument the danios only got caught in the filter because they were ailing and had been sucked in near-dead, but the filter had a weak and badly designed lid and I once observed two fish wriggling through it to get to the water flow.

I bit the bullet and bought a new – much stronger – proprietary internal filter and accepted that I would have to start the filter maturation process from scratch, but this time with fish in my tank right from the beginning.

Of course, the ammonia level quickly spiked, and I undertook 10% water changes every day for the first week. After that, I undertook a 10% water change every other day while my filter continued to mature. While at this point the ammonia level shockingly spiked at 6ppm, the nitrite and nitrate levels also began to rise during the second week, which, although unsettling, was a sign the filter was probably beginning to mature.

I then considered again trying for a bacterial bloom by stopping feeding and water changes. But I couldn't bring myself to do it – my danios had suffered enough. And in any event, I read in a research paper that bacterial blooms are unlikely to occur with *Nitrosomonas* and *Nitrobacter* bacteria and their ilk because they are so slow-growing.

For these reasons, I decided I would mature my tank the slower way by keeping up regular water changes and letting the bacteria gradually establish themselves in my filter over a few weeks. Despite this, the ammonia level continued to spike, although there were still good signs the new filter was maturing nicely because the nitrite and nitrate levels were also still increasing.

If I had been conducting a fishless cycling, I would have continued down this path, but I had to think of my five remaining danios. So I compromised and, after taking further advice, used an ammonia removing solution as a very temporary fix to bring the ammonia level down to 0.5ppm (rather than 0ppm) which I reckoned the danios would tolerate while at the same time providing sufficient ammonia in the tank to continue to feed the *Nitrosomonas* bacteria in the filter maturation process.

In the meantime, I would carry out a 20% water change every day for a fortnight and only feed the fish frugally once each day, gathering up any flakes residue with a net after two minutes' feeding. At the same time, I would put as much biological enhancer, bio balls and plant fertiliser into the tank as I reasonably could without overdosing to enhance the maturation process. I also added a dose of live freshwater bacteria, which to my mind had an almost immediate and astounding positive effect.

Despite this, it would be a nervous wait as the filter fully matured, but hopefully by the end of it I would have a well-cycled tank with five surviving and thriving danios. Miraculously, despite these poor water conditions, I was rewarded at this time by the spawning of two of my egg-scattering danios, who obligingly carved out a hollow in my soil substrate and laid their eggs. So, things can't have been that bad despite everything!

One of the frustrations I encountered at this point in my fishkeeping was that I sought advice on what to do about this emerging dilemma from quite a number of experienced aquarists and they each told me something different. I was told variously to stop water changing for five days while I tried for a bacterial bloom; or to water change 25% every day and forget about a bacterial bloom; or that a bacterial bloom would almost certainly never occur; or to water change 10% every other day while I put a small daily dose of biological enhancer directly into the filter; or that I should use ammonia remover; or that I should *never* use ammonia remover, etc. On and on it went, and I was at risk of becoming completely confused. The solution I eventually came up with comprised a synthesis of what I perceived to be the best and most reasonably prudent of all this advice. I held my heart in my hands for several days. But ultimately it seems to have worked.

It is my strong recollection that none of this was of the slightest concern in the early 1980s. It was explained to me that a lot of modern techniques have been inherited relatively recently – over the past fifteen years or so – from marine fishkeeping. It is quite obvious that we know more about establishing new tanks than we did back then, but I still stand by my recollection that it was not nearly so difficult to establish my old community tank.

I have learned a lot from my experience with my new 40-litre experimental tank. If there's one thing of which I am certain, it's that when I get a much bigger tank in six months or so, I will ensure I have the patience to spend up to twelve weeks adding a little bottled ammonia to a heavily planted tank with no fish in it as I carry out fishless cycling. It seems to me that so-called "fish-in" cycling is generally unnecessary, not only for the suicide squads the subject of it, but also frays the nerves of tropical fish-keepers who love their fish.

Fishless cycling takes a little patience but is not so difficult. It just takes the "artificial" introduction of ammonia to kick start the nitrogen cycle instead of using live fish. The old-fashioned method (still used by some) is to place some dead shrimp into the tank, so its decay creates ammonia. Some aquarists place fish flakes in the water instead. Yet others put in drops of water from a proprietary ammonia bottle (sometimes in combination with fish flakes). Arguably the best method is the ammonia bottle because it is difficult to know precisely how much ammonia is being generated with shrimp or fish flakes, and it is important not to introduce too much (or too little) ammonia because otherwise cycling can be impeded.

I will also concentrate my research on a few select species. This is because I am determined not to have such an eclectic tank as I did in my youth. My first thought about my new bigger tank was to have a pure Amazonian tank with proportionate shoals of neon tetras, cardinal tetras (*Hyphessobrycon cardinalis*) and bronze corys. But my experience with my experimental tank has made me fall in love again with the humble zebra danio, and I insist on having a shoal of those, too.

The bottom line is that my experience suggests fish-in cycling, while almost certainly more speedy than fishless cycling, is ultimately generally unnecessary. It can kill fish if not done properly and also frays the nerves of fish-lovers. With a larger tank, I would rather wait the twelve weeks and buy a bottle of ammonia to precipitate bacterial growth and filter maturation artificially than subject both the fish and I to another cruel and stressful nail-biter.

Call that a failure of nerves if you will. But I will sleep all the better for it – and my fish should thrive.

Appendix 5: Taxonomy of fish species populating 240-litre tank

Zebra danio	
Species	*Danio rerio*
Family	*Cyprinidae*
Size (cm)	≤5
Lifespan (years)	4
Temperature (°c)	17–25
pH	6.2–7.5
Conservation status: Least concern (population decreasing)	

Pepper corys	
Species	*Corydoras paleatus*
Family	*Callichehyldae*
Size (cm)	≤5.9
Lifespan (years)	≤10
Temperature (°c)	20–30
pH	6.5–7.5 in captive bred
Conservation status: Unknown to IUCN Red List as at 20 April 2021	

Glowlight danio	
Species	*Danio choprai*
Family	*Cyprinidae*
Size (cm)	2.5
Lifespan (years)	3
Temperature (°c)	20–24
pH	6.0–7.5
Conservation status: Least Concern (population trend unknown)	

Bronze corys	
Species	*Corydoras aeneus*
Family	*Callichehyldae*
Size (cm)	7
Lifespan (years)	10
Temperature (°c)	20–30
pH	6.5–7.5
Conservation status: Unknown to IUCN Red List as at 20 April 2021	

Gold ring danio	
Species	*Danio tinwini*
Family	*Cyprinidae*
Size (cm)	3
Lifespan (years)	3
Temperature (°c)	18–26
pH	6.5–7.5
Conservation status: Data deficient*	

Amano shrimp	
Species	*Caridina multidentata*
Family	*Atyldae*
Size (cm)	3–6
Lifespan (years)	2–5
Temperature (°c)	18–29
pH	6.0–7.0
Conservation status: Least concern (Population trend unknown)	

Red cherry shrimp	
Species	*Neocaridina Davidi*
Family	*Atyldae*
Size (cm)	4
Lifespan (years)	2
Temperature (°c)	14–29
pH	6.5–8.0
Conservation status: Unknown to IUCN Red List as at 20 April 2021	

Data deficiency: To date it's known only from the Mogaung Chaung (Mogaung stream), Myitkyina District, Kachin State, northern Myanmar, the same watershed to which *D. choprai* is also apparently endemic. This is a tributary of the Irrawaddy/Ayeyarwady River and although the species is probably endemic to the region the possibility that it's been collected from other localities for the aquarium trade cannot be discounted.

Appendix 6: The history of aquariums: A general timeline[30]

Sumarian Fish God carrying ceremonial ritual of water bucket and pine cone

---

30   My sources for this appendix include: Encyclopaedia Britannica, Wikipedia, Ornamental Fishkeeping in Republican and Imperial Rome by Kenneth Wingerter, Piscinae: Artificial Fishponds in Roman Italy by James Higgenbotham, Ancient Egypt, by Eric Brown, Babylon, Mesopotamia and the Birth of Civilization by Paul Kriwaczek, The Babylonians by H.W.F. Suggs, and The Egyptians by Alan Gardiner.

4000–2500BCE: Sumerians and Mesopotamians acknowledge the importance of fish to society and begin to keep freshwater fish in ponds. This appears to have been often for culinary purposes and not always for display. Relevant excerpts from key texts include:

"Oannes, in Mesopotamian mythology, an amphibious being who taught mankind wisdom.... Oannes, as described by the Babylonian priest Berosus, had the form of a fish but with the head of a man under his fish's head and under his fish's tail the feet of a man." (*Britannica*)

"Even slaves ate meat from time to time, but, apart from milk, the only animal protein always widely available on a regular basis was fish. Many kinds are mentioned in documents of the third and early second millennia. A Sumerian text of about 2000 BC describes the habits and appearance of many species of fish in the guise of a deity's invitation to enter the house he has prepared for them, this was probably a piece of scribal erudition which had its basis in more primitive magical spells used by fishermen to charm fish into their nets." (Suggs)

"Because fish were an important part of the diet in the early period, there was need for fishermen in large numbers, and they are duly listed among temple personnel, the temple of the goddess Bau of Lagash alone having more than a hundred. They were divided into fresh-water fishers, sea fishers and fishers in salt waters, the last being those operating in the tidal lagoons of the Tigris and Euphrates." (Suggs)

One can imagine the important symbolic value of fish in Sumerian religion and society, and that attempts were made to "domesticate" freshwater fish in fishponds for food. In his extensive article "Ornamental Fishkeeping in Republican and Imperial Rome", Kenneth Wingerter states that:

"Although he was almost certainly familiar with *earlier histories detailing the establishment of large, artificial fish enclosures in Sumeria,* Egypt, Greece, and Etruscan Italy, Pliny the Elder credits one L. Licinius with the "invention" of the piscina in the early-first century B.C. – as if to say that there were "fishponds" and there were piscinae. Such a distinction would be made not only between Roman and non-Roman fish-keeping practice, but between Roman and non-Roman values and achievements."

This reference to earlier histories would seem to put beyond doubt the contention that the Sumerians almost certainly invented the concept of the artificial freshwater fishpond.

1500BCE: Chinese identify a gold carp as desirable and begin the breeding process from which the goldfish derives.

1279–696BCE: Chinese regularly keep carp and selectively breed them for purely decorative purposes.

Circa 1000BCE: Fish ponds in pleasure gardens constructed by the Ancient Egyptians. Wikipedia explains the position as follows:

> "Ponds and pools were a common feature of the residential gardens of the wealthy and powerful of ancient Egypt, and are shown in a number of tomb paintings. Sometimes, as in the garden of Hatshepsut's mortuary temple at Deir el-Bahri, the pond was in the shape of a T, with one part of the T connected to a river or canal. The water was usually hoisted into the pond from the river by hand, or using a shadouf. Fish for food and ornament were raised in the ponds. They also were the home of migrating water birds."

300BCE–420CE: Large artificial fishponds constructed in Ancient Rome. The arguments in favour of the construction of large artificial fishponds during the Roman supremacy is by now well documented by Kenneth Wingerter in "Ornamental Fishkeeping in Republican and Imperial Rome", and, moreover, by James Higginbotham in his *Piscinae: Artificial Fishponds in Roman Italy*. It would seem that people kept fish as pets as well as for food:

> "The apparent stocking of pet fish (if not the frequent use of costly building materials and of course, apocryphal stories facetiously affirm that fish were not only kept for enjoyment, but that they were oftentimes highly valued. Antonia (mother of emperor Claudius) attached earrings to her favorite eel; the orator Quintus Hortensius is said to have wept over the death of a most prized specimen." (Wingerter)

At the very least, the construction of aquacultural fishponds in ancient Rome was often integrated into the pleasure gardens of villas. So, these fishponds often fulfilled the dual purpose of cultivation and ornament. As James Higgenbotham states in *Piscinae: Artificial Fishponds in Roman Italy*[31]:

> "Most of the fishponds in ancient Italy appear to have been designed so that effective fish raising could be coupled with the pleasure of owning a private body of water replete with aquatic life. Aside from the alimentary uses for fish, the fishpond owner could keep exotic species for show or merely as pets. Piscinae were also built in public and even religious contexts, as evidenced by the ponds in the Palestra at Herculaneum and the sanctuary at Santa Verena outside Paestum. Here, as in the context of a private garden, the fishpond functioned primarily as a decorative element. But in a cultic or religious setting the fish could have served an additional function pertinent to the rites of the cult, serving as cultic symbols of divine prediction."

So, it can be said with some certainty that, in the West at least, Ancient Rome was probably the first society consistently to adopt fish as pets rather than merely as the subjects of aquaculture.

---

31   University of North Carolina Press, 1997 Ed., page 57.

350BCE: There appears to have been activity around aquaculture utilising fishponds in ancient India. In *The Cultural Significance of Fish in India*, Peter Reeves states that: "In the Arahasastra (thought to have been written in the Fourth Century BCE), there is a great deal of evidence that fisheries were carried on: aquaculture in reservoirs was practised; fishery produce and fishermen themselves were taxed..."

There is also evidence that in ancient India ornamental fishponds existed at the fronts of temples: As in ancient Sumaria, gods in the form of fish were common, and indeed Vishnu has a fish form.[32]

265–1279CE: During this period great strides were made by the Chinese in ornamental fishkeeping. In a paper entitled "Goldfish: From Tang Dynasty Ponds to 21st Century Aquariums"[33], Jonathan DeHart explains that:

"Sometime during the Jin Dynasty (265–42CE) the ancient Chinese observed that some of the freshwater carp they were breeding as food fish tended to occasionally display mutated colors ranging from red to orange and yellow. A few centuries later, those living during the artistically inclined Tang Dynasty (618–907) began to develop ornamental water gardens which they stocked with a gold variation of the silver Prussian carp, from which goldfish sprang (from the Cyprinidae family of the Cyprinoid order). During social gatherings, some of the finer specimens were temporarily showcased in smaller containers – the world's first fish tanks – to show off to guests. By the Song Dynasty (960-1279) this practice was commonplace."

Charlemagne and the Middle Ages: There is considerable evidence of the sporadic establishing of fishponds in the Middle Ages. Wikipedia states:

"Records of the use of fishponds can be found from the early Middle Ages. The idealized 8th-century estate of Charlemagne's *capitulary de villis* was to have artificial fishponds but, 200 years later, facilities for raising fish remained very rare, even on monastic estates. As the Middle Ages progressed, fishponds became a more common feature of urbanizing environments."

There was a significant tradition of monastic houses building and managing fishponds throughout Europe in the Medieval period and during the Middle Ages. So, in the British context, Historic England[34] categorises two monastic fishpond sites: one at North Kelsey Grange in Lincolnshire and the other at Park House in North Yorkshire. Of the Lincolnshire site, Historic England states that:

"The tradition of constructing and using fishponds in England began during the medieval period and peaked in the 12th century. They were largely built by the wealthy sectors of society with monastic institutions and royal residences often having large and complex fishponds. The difficulties of obtaining fresh meat in the winter and the value placed on fish as a food source and for status

---

32   See for instance *Fish in Indian Folklore and the Age of Atharvareda* by A.P. Kamarnar (1947).
33   The Diplomat, 9 October 2013.
34   www.historicengland.org.uk.

may have been factors which favoured the development of fishponds and which made them so valuable. The practice of constructing fishponds declined after the Dissolution of the Monasteries in the 16th century although in some areas it continued into the 17th century. Most fishponds fell out of use during the post-medieval period although some were re-used as ornamental features in 19th and early 20th century landscape parks or gardens, or as watercress beds. Documentary sources provide a wealth of information about the way fishponds were stocked and managed. The main species of fish kept were eel, tench, pickerel, bream, perch, and roach. Large quantities of fish could be supplied at a time... Although approximately 2000 examples are recorded nationally, this is thought to be only a small proportion of those in existence in medieval times."

Circa 500–1500CE: Fishponds recorded in Muslim and Persian texts. Terry Allen, in his paper "An Amasid Fishpond Villa Near Marrah"[35], observes that:

"There must be many references in early Arabic literature to fish in water and ponds. The Birkah al-Ja'farīyah at Samarra was eulogized by the poet al-Walīd b. 'Ubayd al-Buhturī, who mentioned fish swimming in it. Ahmad Sūsah locates the Birkah al-Ja'farīyah at the palace known as al-Musharrahāt, according to Alastair Northedge, who finds "no particular reason to locate" it there. There is a reservoir about two hundred meters square at al-Musharrahāt, which Northedge plausibly characterizes as a hunting palace because of the adjoining game reserve in which the reservoir itself is located...

Al-Maqqarī mentions fishponds (buhayrāt) containing fish (hītān) at Madīnah al-Zahra' and that the fish were fed bread and chickpeas, but does not describe the shape or features of the ponds. A reservoir that very likely was a fishpond was excavated near Cordoba in 1910 by Ricardo Velázquez Bosco... This reservoir, built of ashlar, is trapezoidal, nearly fifty meters long, an average of twenty-eight meters wide, and four meters deep; it could be filled to a depth of 3.85 meters. It might well have been filled to a somewhat shallower level. The reservoir's remarkable feature is a walkway all around its circumference, corbelled out over the body of the reservoir on a series of shallow barrel vaults. Velázquez Bosco thought this walkway implied recreational use and likened the reservoir to others in Persian palaces, in the Alhambra (the Court of the Myrtles and the Partal), the fishponds at Madīnah al-Zahra', and that in the Dār al-Bahr in the Qal'ah of the Banū Hammād."

Islamic gardens were popular at this time throughout the Muslim world including Persia and Mughal India[36], and regularly featured pools the design of which had significant symbolic value. Evidence of the stocking of fish in such ancient pools seems scanty, perhaps because the architects did not want to detract from their historic symbolic value and their fundamental importance as still, reflective spaces, and because the water flowing through them was often used as a drinking

---

35 Solipsist Press, California, 2009.
36 See for instance the Islamic gardens at the Taj Mahal and the Shah-Gil Garden, Tabriz.

source. It is evident however that the stocking of contemporary Islamic gardens with ornamental fish was probably permitted. Perhaps more primary research could be done in this context.

1365–1694: During the Ming Dynasty breeders experiment further with raising fish in tanks indoors.

1600s: Samuel Pepys refers to fish being kept in a bowl and describes them as *"exceedingly fine"*. There is evidence that goldfish were being regularly successfully kept in glass vessels in England by the 1750s.

1805: Robert Warrington is credited with studying the oxygen, plant and animal cycle in a tank and maintaining one of the first stable tanks.

1832: Naturalist Jeanne Villepreaux-Power invents the first glass aquarium.

1851: Great Exhibition starts an aquarium fad.

1853: First public aquarium is opened in London at Regent's Park Zoological Gardens (followed by aquariums in Berlin, Naples and Paris).

1854: Phillip Gosse publishes his book *"The Aquarium: An Unveiling of the Wonders of the Deep Water"*, in which the word "aquarium" is probably used for the first time. He defines it as a vessel in which aquatic animals, as well as plants, can be held.

1858: Glass-fronted aquarium patented by Edward Edwards.

1908: First mechanical air pump invented.

1920s: Electricity establishes the viability of electric heaters, filters and air pumps.

1950s: Plastic shopping and packing bags introduced, making it easier to import fish.

1980s: Takashi Amano invents the art of "Aquascaping".

1996: Keeping aquariums is the second most popular hobby in the US after stamp collecting.

Post-1980s: Nitrogen cycle identified as essential to an understanding of tropical freshwater fishkeeping.

2020: Research suggests that 14% of households in the United Kingdom keep fish as pets.

Select bibliography

The Perfect Aquarium, Jeremy Gay (Hamlyn, 2005 Ed.)

The Aquarium Masterclass (Practical Fishkeeping, API and Aquarian)

Aquascaping, George Farmer (Sports Publishing, 2020 Ed.)

The Ecology of the Planted Aquarium, Diana L. Walstad (Echinodorus, 3rd Ed.)

Freshwater Aquariums for Dummies, Madelaine Frances Heleine (Dummies Series, 3rd Ed.)

Danio Care – The Complete Guide to Caring For and Keeping Danios as Pet Fish, Tabitha Jones (2019 Ed.)

All About Tropical Fish, Derek McInerny and Geoffrey Gerard (Harrap, 1980 Ed.)

Do Fish Feel Pain?, Dr Victoria Braithwaite (Oxford University Press, 2010 Ed.)

What a Fish Knows: The Inner Lives of Our Underwater Cousins, by Jonathan Balcombe (Oneworld, 2016 Ed.)

Fishes: An Introduction to Ichthyology, Peter Moyle and Joseph Cech (Prentice Hall)

Fish Cognition and Behavior, by Culum Brown et al (Blackwell Publishing, 2006)

Piscinae: Artificial Fishponds in Roman Italy, James Higgenbotham (University of North Carolina Press, 2012 Ed.)

The World's Forgotten Fishes Report, WWF et al (March 2021)

Practical Fishkeeping Magazine, Editor Nathan Hill (Every month)

Tropical Fish Hobbyist Magazine, Editor Albert Connolly Jr (Every two months)

UK Aquatic Plant Society Forum (www.ukaps.org)

IUCN Red List (Red List citations in this edition are valid as at 20 April 2021)

TheSprucePets.com website (www.thesprucepets.com)

Maidenhead Aquatics website (www.fishkeeper.co.uk)

Wikipedia

Encyclopaedia Britannica

List of images

1. Leopard danio *(Danio rerio)*..3
2. Cardinal tetras in shoal *(Paracheirodon axelrodi)*...........................5
3. Black moly *(Poecilia sphenops)*...9
4. Green cabomba *(Cabomba caroliniana)*...12
5. A typical crypt *(Cryptocoryne wendtii)*...13
6. Amazon sword plant *(Echinodorus bleheri)*..................................14
7. Zebra danios in shoal *(Danio rerio)*..18
8. My 40 litre tank after cycling..21
9. Amano shrimp *(Caridina multidentate)*..22
10. Leopard corydoras *(Corydoras leopardus)*....................................23
11. Transcript of the commencement of 'Aquarium' from 'The Carnival of the Animals', by Camille Saint-Saëns (1886)..........................28
12. Wucai fish jar from British Museum (1567–1572)........................29
13. 'Goldfish', by Sanyu (1895–1966)...30
14. 'Fish', by James Prosek (Circa 2019)...30
15. 'Still Life of Fish', by Abraham van Beyeren (circa 1655)............31
16. 'Purposeful Ichthus by Two', by J. Vincent Scarpace (1971–)......32
17. 'Scripture Fish', by J. Vincent Scarpace (1971–).............................32
18. The coelacanth *(Coelacanthiformes)*..40
19. The Amazon River..42
20. 'God creating the birds and the fishes', by Martin de Vos (1532-1603)......48
21. Zebra Danio *(Danio rerio)*..52
22. International Space Station...53
23. Zebra danios shoaling...54
24. Bronze corydoras *(Corydoras aenous)*..59
25. Blue danio *(Danio kerri)*..61
26. Gold ring danio *(Danio tinwini)*..63
27. Glowlight danio *(Danio choprai)*...66
28. A brilliant Aquascape...70
29. Cat with fish in its eyes..72
30. 'Salute to the Zebra Danios', by Robert Porter.............................74
31. Red cherry shrimp *(Neocaridina davidi)*......................................77
32. Sumarian Fish God carrying ceremonial ritual of water bucket and pine cone.....111

Most images are used under licence from Shutterstock and Adobe Stock.

List of figures

1. Equipment purchased for experimental 40-litre tank and its cycling 13
2. Fish purchased for experimental 40-litre tank 16
3. Fluval New Roma 240-litre tank..57
4. Species selection for new 240-litre tank...60
5. Proportionate analysis of fish stock for new 240-litre tank.......................60
6. Range and habitat of selected Danio species 64
7. Map showing the general distribution of the genus Danio 64
8. Non-exclusive equipment list for new 240-litre tank...............................65
9. Example ammonia (NH_3), nitrite (NO_2) and nitrate (NO_3) fluctuations during a fishless cycle (with bacteria growth encouraged by the addition of live bacteria) using an API liquid test kit..68
10. Daily feeding regimen for moderately-stocked 40-litre tank 79
11. Chemicals added to 40-litre tank on 20% water change twice weekly.......82
12. Proposed purchases for possible 240-litre tank..94
13. Specimen selection of plants for proposed 240-litre tank.........................95

Acknowledgements

In writing a book there are inevitably a considerable number of people who have helped. Some one has known for years, perhaps all one's life. Some one has met along the way in the editorial process. Some are interested in tropical freshwater fish, others couldn't care less.

The first people I would like to thank are my parents, Beezer and Margaret, who bought me my first fish tank when I was thirteen and introduced me to the hobby. I would also like to thank my sister, Kate, who hated my fish and kept telling me they freaked her out, but who endured them as an act of love towards me.

From all those years ago, I would also like to thank the proprietors of Grosvenor Aquatics on the Woodstock Road in Belfast, who sold me my first fish and guided me on my way. Brian Whiteside, of the *Aquarist and Pondkeeper,* deserves thanks for publishing my aquarist's letter to him in August 1980, which not only encouraged me considerably as a fishkeeper, but also comprised my first ever publishing success in life.

Effusive thanks to the Rt Hon Chris Smith, Lord Smith of Finsbury, for writing the foreword to this book and for all his encouragement and support.

Considerable thanks must go to Al Connelly Jr, editor of *Tropical Fish Hobbyist Magazine*, for having the faith in me as an aquarist to publish my first comprehensive fishkeeping article.

Many thanks to Henry Howard Sneyd, Chairman of Asian Art, Europe and Americas at Sotheby's, Robin Nicholson, formerly Director of the Telfair Museums in Savanna, Georgia and now an Art Museum Strategic Consultant, Dr Colin Wilcockson, Fellow of Pembroke College, Cambridge, and Philip Godfrey ARCO, for their insights and advice into the Artistic, literary and musical aspects relating to freshwater fishkeeping.

Huge thanks to Susan Cunningham MA VetMB MRCVS, Michael Brown CBE MVO, Dana Ammaday, Rev Rory MacLeod, Kate Baird, Mark Dunfoy and Andrew McClean for reading and commenting on the penultimate draft. Their input has been invaluable.

Many thanks to Rupert Butler and Colin Howes for giving legal advice around this book, in particular with regard to the applicability of the Animal Welfare Act 2006 to tropical freshwater fish.

My thanks to my good friend Mick Mullally for all his support with some of the practical DIY aspects of fishkeeping. Few know as he does (apart perhaps from my wife!) how unhandy I am with a screwdriver.

Great thanks to my very good and lifelong friend Peter McCalister for vetting and approving my bagpipe 4/4 *Salute to the Zebra Danios*.

Thanks to Nathan Hill, editor of *Practical Fishkeeping Magazine*, for all his friendly and helpful advice, and for introducing me to that little Danio gem, *Danio tinwini*.

Many thanks to the teams at Maidenhead Aquatics, Morden and Pets at Home, Putney who have cheerfully sold me endless fishes and aquarists' products and put up with my seemingly idiotic questions as they advised me in the early days.

Profound thanks must go to David Mogg for typesetting and formatting my manuscript and for designing the cover.

Immense thanks to Stephanie Farrow for proofreading and generally sanity-checking the document, and for the diligent provision of ongoing publishing advice.

A huge thank you to J. Vincent Scarpace for granting his gracious permission to use his quite beautiful and impactful painting Purposeful Ichthus by Two on the front cover. And also for devoting his life to creating such amazing artistic depictions of fish - the world is a better place for it.

Thanks to Dana Ammaday for giving me robust advice about the marketing of this book, and for being a wonderful mentor and support in the publishing process. Thanks, too, to Kate Lyall Grant for similar support and for general ongoing publishing advice and friendship.

Grateful thanks, too, to Johnny and Susan Cunningham, Mike and Ali McNeil and Rupert Morley for offering their help towards the publication of this book.

Perhaps the deepest thanks must go to my family. They have put up with my vagaries and eccentricities around fish as they wondered what all the fuss was about. But I have been rewarded by watching them observe the development of my tank with interest, so perhaps I have a few new aquarists in the making. In particular I owe a debt of gratitude to my wife for giving me the benefit of the doubt against her better judgement and allowing my experimental 40-litre tank over the threshold. Without that concession I would never have rediscovered fishkeeping and never written this book. It has all given me great happiness.

Finally, and perhaps most eccentrically, thanks must go to my humble zebra danios. For being such beautiful yet hardy fish. For bringing me such joy. A special feast of daphnia for you this evening!

About the author

Originally from Belfast, Robert Porter is a former barrister and solicitor who lives in London, UK. He was a Consultant and Head of the Charities Group at the renowned media and entertainment law firm Harbottle & Lewis LLP where he acted for numerous clients including Richard Branson, Virgin Group, Fujitsu-ICL, Comic Relief, The Diana, Princess of Wales Memorial Fund, The Prince's Trust and The Royal Household.

Robert has advised on a number of environmental and conservation projects and was a representative at the 1998 CITES Animals Committee Conference in Caracas, where he worked closely with WWF and the Species Survival Network. Robert was a trustee of the Kasanka Trust for many years, a conservation charity that part funds Kasanka National Park in Zambia. Robert was also a trustee of Shelter (the Housing Charity) for five years and is a Fellow of the Royal Geographical Society.

Robert has kept freshwater tropical fish on and off since he was thirteen. He has at least one article scheduled for publication in *Tropical Fish Hobbyist* in 2022 and is an occasional contributor to *The Irish Times*.

Robert writes screenplays, and currently has two in development, one about environmental issues and another about surfing and mental health.

Robert is married with two children, two cats and a tankful of tropical fish.

Printed in Great Britain
by Amazon